Pottery Function

A Use-Alteration
Perspective

INTERDISCIPLINARY CONTRIBUTIONS TO ARCHAEOLOGY

THE AMERICAN SOUTHWEST AND MESOAMERICA
Systems of Prehistoric Exchange
Edited by Jonathon E. Ericson and Timothy G. Baugh

ECOLOGY AND HUMAN ORGANIZATION ON THE GREAT PLAINS
Douglas B. Bamforth

ETHNOHISTORY AND ARCHAEOLOGY
Approaches to Post-Contact Change in the Americas
Edited by J. Daniel Rogers and Samuel M. Wilson

FROM KOSTENKI TO CLOVIS
Upper Paleolithic–Paleoindian Adaptations
Edited by Olga Soffer and N. D. Praslov

HOLOCENE HUMAN ECOLOGY IN NORTHEASTERN NORTH AMERICA
Edited by George P. Nicholas

HUNTER–GATHERERS
Archaeological and Evolutionary Theory
Robert L. Bettinger

THE INTERPRETATION OF ARCHAEOLOGICAL SPATIAL PATTERNING
Edited by Ellen M. Kroll and T. Douglas Price

THE PLEISTOCENE OLD WORLD: Regional Perspectives
Edited by Olga Soffer

POTTERY FUNCTION
A Use-Alteration Perspective
James M. Skibo

RESOURCES, POWER, AND INTERREGIONAL INTERACTION
Edited by Edward M. Schortman and Patricia A. Urban

SPACE, TIME, AND ARCHAEOLOGICAL LANDSCAPES
Edited by Jacqueline Rossignol and LuAnn Wandsnider

Pottery Function

A Use-Alteration Perspective

JAMES M. SKIBO

Illinois State University
Normal, Illinois

PLENUM PRESS • *NEW YORK AND LONDON*

Library of Congress Cataloging-in-Publication Data

Skibo, James M.
    Pottery function : a use-alteration perspective / James M. Skibo.
        p.   cm. -- (Interdisciplinary contributions to archaeology)
    Includes bibliographical references and index.
    ISBN 0-306-44159-4
    1. Kalinga (Philippine people)--Antiquities.   2. Pottery-
-Philippines--Guinaang--Themes, motives.   3. Pottery--Philippines-
-Guinaang--Analysis.   4. Ethnoarchaeology--Philippines--Guinaang.
5. Guinaang (Philippines)--Antiquities.   6. Philippines-
-Antiquities.   I. Title.   II. Series.
DS666.K3S55   1992
959.9--dc20   92-13591
                                                                   CIP

ISBN 0-306-44159-4

© 1992 Plenum Press, New York
A Division of Plenum Publishing Corporation
233 Spring Street, New York, N.Y. 10013

Printed in the United States of America

Foreword

There are many ways to study pots or the sherds of pots. In this book James Skibo has focused on the surface wear and tear found on the resin-coated, low-fired cooking pots of the Kalinga people in north-western Luzon. This detailed analysis is part of a much larger evaluation of Kalinga pottery production and use by the staff members and students at the University of Arizona that has been underway since 1972. Here he has analyzed the variants among the possible residual clues on pots that have endured the stresses of having been used for cooking meat and vegetables or rice; standing on supports in the hearth fire; wall scrapings while distributing the food; being transported to the water source for thorough washing and scrubbing; followed by storage until needed again—a repetitive pattern of use. This well-controlled study made use of new pots provided for cooking purposes to one Kalinga household, as well as those pots carefully observed in other households—189 pots in all. Such an ethnoarchaeological approach is not unlike following the course of the firing of a kiln-load of pots in other cultures, and then purchasing the entire product of this firing for analysis. Other important aspects of this Kalinga study are the chemical analysis of extracts from the ware to deduce the nature of the food cooked in them, and the experimental study of soot deposited on cooking vessels when they are in use.

This volume is specifically addressed to archaeologists working with low-fired wares. It is obvious that those working in geological and cultural areas other than Luzon must review this report in terms of their own problems. For instance, there are great differences in the working and firing behavior of clays in many parts of the world. Thermal alteration of the bits of limestone that occurs in many clays can result in disastrous spalling, quite different in cause and appearance from the steam-induced spalls reported by Skibo in his essentially lime-free clay. The nature of an intermittent or continuous reducing or oxidizing atmosphere during firing must also be kept in mind as well as the type of clay and fuel when studying soot deposits and carbon cores. Potters can have great flexibility in their methods of ware production and these are often influenced by social constraints. For instance, the death of a potter, the nature of the cooperating household, the products of children with their small hands, the time demands of compulsory schooling today, and economic imperatives such as the cost of fuel and clay procurement, heavy rains, or changes in market demands, can quickly alter production techniques and even vessel shapes and sizes. More elusive aspects such as consumers' attitudes toward the potters and the products of competitive villages— "the food (or water) doesn't taste right" from certain wares when purchases are made in the market—must be kept in mind. It is obvious, but perhaps needs stating, that ceramic archaeologists must collaborate with colleagues knowledgeable in the technological aspects of clay properties when making their deductions or assumptions, let alone their interpretations. It is also helpful when they listen to the comments of their local village workmen with respect to the uses of the vessels they unearth. Skibo is indeed fortunate in being a key member of a broadly based ceramic team. The breadth of its interests can be quickly seen in a recent study (Longacre, Skibo, and Stark 1991).

Potsherds have served as the equivalent of laboratory animals in the study of past cultures and civilizations. The shapes and sizes of vessels, together with their decoration applied in so many different ways, have long been used as indicators of cultural change, foreign influence or trade, technological development, and so forth without diminishing their appeal as artistic objects for exhibit in museums. Beginning in the 1920s, perhaps a little earlier, the less than perfect or attractive vessels and sherds, possibly cooking pots, that had been retained by the excavators began to receive more attention. The ways in which they were studied differed with the investigators and with the nature of the materials excavated. The ceramic problems being addressed greatly influenced the extent of the analyses. Skibo's study demonstrates that there are still new approaches that can be undertaken in pottery analyses, in this case of the usually neglected cooking pots that have seen much use and abuse.

As archaeologists we should give more care as to how our potsherds are retrieved and cleaned so as to preserve clues found in marks of abrasion and attrition. Low-fired sherds long buried in moist soils frequently have soft surfaces that are easily scratched by scrubbing brushes. Yet when such sherds are allowed to dry in the sun before being washed they harden permanently and do not soften in the scrub water. This reaction of low-fired clay, partial rehydration during long burial with some resumption of its original colloidal properties followed by a semi-permanent set when again dry, is fascinating but is archaeologically dangerous. Soft surfaces can be altered when cleaned, and decorative pigment may be removed. Some of us working at early sites in the Near East, where red-slipped and red-decorated pottery occurs, tell those washing the ware, "If you see blood in the wash water, STOP!" For one using pots and sherds when searching for information about ancient food preparation, diets, agricultural practices, deforestation, and so forth, it is essential that adequate control be exercised over local workmen and students who clean the pottery first in the field and again in the laboratory.

It is fascinating and satisfying to observe the newer interest of students of ancient pottery, now often rightly termed ceramic ethno-archaeologists, as they continue to use their materials to reconstruct life in the past in its physical and social aspects. They are often aided when they take the time to study local pottery, brick, and roof tile production in the region in which they are working. We can always learn and apply concepts or archaeometric approaches used by colleagues working in other geographic and time regions, particularly if our cultural blinders do not hinder broader bibliographic ceramic interests. I hope that Skibo's work will be of use to those who are studying potters still working within their craft traditions even though they sell their shape-modified wares to tourists. Archaeologists, I trust, can become better aware of the potential value of the close study of their cooking pots. I know that in my continuing studies of low-fired pottery used in the early village-farming communities of the Near East during the seventh and sixth millennia B.C.E. I shall now approach my sherds with new questions, and I hope look at them constructively in more meticulous detail.

There may be still unexplored ways in which pottery can be used to learn more about humans. It has been observed that pots are fragile but potsherds last forever. I wonder how our successors will make better use of them?

FREDERICK R. MATSON

Research Professor Emeritus of Archaeology
The Pennsylvania State University
University Park, Pennsylvania

Preface

Beginning in 1987, ethnoarchaeological research among the Kalinga was resumed under the direction of William A. Longacre. This provided me with the opportunity to see pottery in use and to observe some of the processes that previously I had only been able to infer from excavation or through experimentation. The experience changed forever the way I look at archaeological material.

Because only a few archaeologists are able to perform research among living groups, it is imperative that we ethnoarchaeologists report our findings in a way that will be of some use to those left to draw inferences from buried sherds and trash middens. This is not always easy. Too often, ethnoarchaeological data and information recovered from excavation are incompatible. There is often a disjunction between units of analysis and observation in prehistory and ethnoarchaeology. Although the prehistorian can do much to alleviate this problem, it is the objective of this study—and indeed the entire Kalinga Ethnoarchaeological Project—to provide information that will be of direct use to many archaeologists.

A pottery use-alteration study, I believe, is one area that can have direct application to archaeological material. A major inspiration for this project is the weak link in many archaeological inferences based on pottery: Too often there is little or no information about how the pottery was used.

In all of archaeology, we are wont to create often grandiose scenarios based on variability or change of various pottery attributes, but we make many of these inferences on very soft footing. It is difficult—if not impossible—to understand why there was a change in a pottery decorative style or technological attribute if there is little information about how the pots were used in everyday life. It is the primary purpose of this study to provide the archaeologist with the means to determine actual pottery use.

This study has several objectives. First, as did lithic use-wear research pioneered over 20 years ago, I hope this study will provide pottery analysts with a useful tool. This study is not just a description of use traces on Kalinga pottery, it is a discussion of the processes that result in chemical residues, attrition, and carbon deposits and the tools for analyzing them. I will consider this study a success if the pottery analyst, armed with this information, is able to infer more accurately pottery use from traces that remain on vessels or sherds.

Second, I provide archaeologists—even those not directly interested in use alteration—with a description of household pottery use. This is the first ethnoarchaeological study that focuses on pottery use, and the detailed discussion will provide the archaeologist a glimpse at some of the many household pottery use activities.

A final objective is to discuss, from a theoretical perspective, the role of ethnoarchaeology and experimental studies in archaeological inference. Although there has been much recent ethnoarchaeological and experimental work, we lack current statements about how each field is defined and how they fit into archaeological inference. This discussion will interest archaeologists who are interested in method and theory.

The Pasil River Valley was the perfect place to conduct this research. All the households in Guina-ang, without exception, gave us complete access to their homes. Partly because the Kalinga are generally warm and friendly and partly because of Longacre's long-standing relationship with the people of the Pasil Valley, we were permitted not only to count and measure all household pots but also to inventory personal possessions and conduct a census. Although our questions and general behavior may have seemed strange, I thank the people of Guina-ang for waiting (usually) until we left their houses before laughing.

Our assistants in Guina-ang deserve special thanks for making our stay both productive and safe. They include Amboy Lingbawan, Joseph Abacan, Nancy Lugao, Edita Lugao, Judith Sagayo, and our cook, Iya Lubuagon. In addition, John and Delia Sawil, Thomasa Dawagan and family, Anastasio Latawan, Solano Latawan and family, Francisco Mani-ag and family, the Amangan family, Roberto and Christina Tima (of Dang-talan), and the Awing family (Dalupa) made our stay more pleasant. Finally, I thank the young men of Guina-ang for our most enjoyable and interesting games of basketball.

The manuscript for this book was a revised version of my doctoral dissertation. My committee members—Michael B. Schiffer, William A. Longacre (cochairs), Carol Kramer, and David Kingery—deserve thanks for their support and for letting me write a book instead of a "disserta-tion." I am especially indebted to Mike Schiffer and Bill Longacre; al-though I can never repay them, I hope that they are aware that this study would not have been possible without their support. Many never get a chance to have one wonderful mentor; I was blessed with two. I wish to single out three other individuals for their contribution to my work. David Hally's ceramic work was an inspiration, and he provided me with comments and advice throughout. The residue analysis was improved significantly by knowing Michael Deal; he not only provided me with comments but also graciously shared references and unpublished data. Finally, Paul Fish deserves thanks for providing me with many research opportunities and access to archaeological material.

Numerous friends, colleagues, and members of our writers group con-tributed greatly to this study. They include (alphabetically) Walt Allen, Meredith Aronson, Charles Bollong, Trixi Bubemyre, Cathy Cameron, Jeff Clark, Chris Downum, Kelley Hays, Masashi Kobayashi (codirector of the pottery use study), Laura Levi, Jon Mabry, Barb Montgomery, Mark Neupert, Axel Nielsen, Barb Roth, Ramon Silvestre, Miriam Stark, Al Sullivan, Chris Szuter, Masa Tani, Brian Trostel, Chris Turner, Mary Van Buren, Jose L. Villamor, William Walker, John Welch, Steve West, Lisa Young, and Nieves Zedeno. Barbara Montgomery drafted Figures 4.3, 6.1, 6.11, 7.1, and 7.2, and Arnel Delfin of Dangtalan made the original drawing of Figure 4.3.

Three National Science Foundation awards supported my research. Data collection was supported by funds (BNS-87-10275) awarded to W. A. Longacre, the analysis was funded by a dissertation improvement grant (BNS-89-15359), and laboratory and analytical research money came from two grants (BNS-86-46597 and BNS-89-01797) awarded to M. B. Schiffer. The Laboratory of Traditional Technology, the National Museum of the Philippines, and the University of the Philippines, Quezon City, also offered support and assistance.

Finally, I thank my family. My parents and sisters have unfailingly supported my work. Becky—my wife and best friend—has been beside me through it all, and Matthew, our son, helps keep life in proper perspective. Because of Becky's endless support and love, I dedicate this work to her.

Contents

Chapter **1**

Introduction

> The investigation should begin with ethnographic analysis of wear on [ceramic] pieces whose use . . . is observable or documented. (Chernela 1969:177)

The task for the archaeologist is difficult. Broken pottery, crumbled buildings, and other fragmentary items are not the best sources of information for reconstructing the past. Not only is the relationship between material items and behavior complicated, but the material record is often incomplete and nonrepresentative. Throughout the history of archaeology, this situation has resulted in interpretations about the past that range from wild speculation to very conservative and uninformative reconstructions. But this situation has also stimulated research that investigates directly the relationship between material culture and human behavior. In this context, ethnoarchaeology and experimental archaeology have become important for strengthening archaeological inference. The overall objective of each subfield is to provide the means whereby the prehistorian can more accurately connect activities of the past with their material residues. Both ethnoarchaeology and experimental archaeology are employed in the present study to investigate a recurring question in prehistoric reconstructions: *How was pottery used?* The research discussed here focuses on demonstrating links between the contents of pottery vessels, activities of use, and the resultant alterations to the ceramic body.

The current interest in pottery utilization can be traced to Matson (1965:202-217), who introduced an approach to ceramic analysis that he termed *ceramic ecology*. He advocated that archaeologists focus on how pottery was made and used rather than on cultural-historical reconstructions. The orientation of this research can also be linked to Shepard's (1965) early work on the physical properties of pottery. The importance of their research, however, was not immediately realized; few individuals employ this new strategy, and their analyses were usually relegated to appendices of archaeological reports (see Cordell 1991; Crown 1991; De Atley and Bishop 1991, for a discussion of the reasons behind the lack of integration of such work into mainstream archaeology). In American archaeology, it was not until the 1980s that Matson's approach to ceramic analysis became more widely employed. Although a number of individuals began earlier to consider seriously the relationship between ceramic technology and use (e.g., Ericson *et al.* 1972; Shepard 1965), the contributions of Braun (1980, 1983) signaled a new orientation for ceramic studies. Braun (1983:107) advocates that archaeologists should view "pots as tools" and notes that many of the attributes commonly recorded for classificatory purposes can inform on how the potter may have manufactured the vessel for a particular use.

There has now been a rapid acceleration of studies that focus on reconstructing how a pottery vessel was used and how the potter may have designed the pot to best suit that use (see Rice 1987:207-242; Sinopoli 1991:9-42). But unlike research with prehistoric stone tools, there has not been a systematic study of ceramic use-wear. Like lithic use-wear studies, alteration of *pottery* as a result of activity can inform directly on how the vessel was utilized in the past. The overall objective of my research is to provide a framework of ceramic alteration (use and nonuse) that will permit archaeologists to exploit use-alteration information for making inferences about pottery function.

Understanding how pottery was used is important for several reasons (see also Rice 1990; Schiffer 1989:184-186). First, virtually all inferences about past society based on pottery demand a clear understanding about pottery function (i.e., socio-, ideo-, and technofunction—defined in Chapter 3). On the most general level, pottery assemblages are frequently used to draw inferences about prehistoric diet, demography, trade, social complexity, and social change, to name a few. The core of such inferences is an accurate assessment of how the pottery was used. As such, archaeological inferences will improve with better methods for determining pottery use. For example, reconstructions of prehistoric social organization in the American Southwest, based on pottery use (cf. Upham 1982), could be improved if there was specific information about how pottery functioned in Puebloan society. Moreover, demographic estimates based upon pottery would be more accurate with specific pottery use information; though ethnographic households have many pots, only those used for daily cooking may reflect household size (cf. Nelson 1981; Tani n.d.; Turner and Lofgren 1966).

Second, if pottery is considered a tool, it is imperative that archaeologists be able to reconstruct accurately how people used their ceramic vessels. It is now known that potters manipulated, in many cases, attributes such as temper, surface treatment, or form, to suit a particular use (e.g., Skibo *et al.* 1989a; Smith 1985). Further advances in this area of study will result only if ways are developed to make pottery use inferences with much finer resolution. For example, it would be difficult to explain a change in a physical attribute, such as temper or morphology of the vessel, without knowing how people were using the pot in everyday life.

Third, it has been demonstrated that the household is both a convenient and appropriate analytic unit from which to investigate past society (e.g., Stanish 1989; Wilk and Rathje 1982). The study of household-specific activities involving pottery would benefit from an accurate means of inferring pottery use. Further, inferences regarding site function and activity areas would attain a finer level of resolution if pottery use could be expressed more accurately.

Fourth, pottery use influences greatly pottery use life and the formation, ultimately, of the archaeological assemblage (see Longacre *et al.* 1988; Mills 1989; Nelson 1991; Tani n.d.). Vessels used in different contexts and for varying purposes will have different use lives, and, consequently, will enter archaeological context at equally dissimilar rates. Because all archaeological inference based on pottery is reliant on this transformation, it is imperative that an accurate determination of pottery use can be made.

Finally, the study of pottery style will be enhanced by more accurate means to determine pottery use (Braun 1983:113; Plog 1980:85-89; Schiffer 1989:185). On the most general level, pottery used in different contexts will often be decorated differently. For example, pottery used in daily cooking may have different painted designs than vessels used in villagewide celebrations even if the same food items are cooked. Methods to determine how pottery was used would improve our ability to make inferences, based on ceramics, about virtually all aspects of past behavior.

The primary data for this study are an ethnographic collection of used pottery recovered as part of the Kalinga Ethnoarchaeological Project (see Longacre and Skibo n.d.). Pottery use was observed in a Kalinga village, and nearly 200 used vessels were transported to Tucson and are now housed in the Arizona State Museum. (Details of the field research are provided in Chapter 4.) This is the largest known ethnographic assemblage of used pottery for which there is detailed information about pottery use. Linking the pottery use activity with the resultant modifications to the vessel serves as the basis for this study. In several cases in which the link was unclear between pottery use and vessel alteration, experiments were performed.

To place this research in the proper theoretical context, Chapters 2 and 3 discuss definitions of ethnoarchaeology and experimental archaeology and provide a framework for the study of use alteration. In the past decade many have used ethnoarchaeological and experimental approaches to explore a particular question in prehistory, but there have been few attempts at defining the two subfields and placing them in the broader context of archaeological inference. Chapter 2 provides a discussion of these issues and argues that ethnoarchaeology and experimental archaeology pursue the same objective but differ in the control over variables and in the type of data each subfield can analyze. It is also demonstrated, with a case study, that many questions in prehistory can be addressed by combining these two approaches.

In Chapter 3 the various methods for inferring pottery function are reviewed. Intended and actual pottery use are contrasted, and it is argued that only ceramic use-alteration research can reconstruct *actual* pottery use, which is often what is needed in archaeological inference. The chapter concludes with a description of a framework for ceramic alteration. Drawing from the lithic use-wear literature, this framework includes all forms of ceramic alteration (use and nonuse), beginning with vessel manufacture until recovery by the archaeologist.

The Kalinga Ethnoarchaeological Project is introduced in Chapter 4. A general description of the Kalinga is provided, and present and former research on this group is described. Guina-ang, home for the ceramic use-alteration study, is described as is the general method of Kalinga pottery manufacture. The field research strategy is discussed; it included intensive observations of pottery use, a complete household pottery inventory, household census, and a collection of household economic data.

Methods of pottery collection and transport are also described. The final section of this chapter discusses the general pattern of Kalinga pottery use.

Chapters 5, 6, and 7 discuss the results of the pottery analyses. Chapter 5 describes the residue study. After a review of the various forms of residue analysis, a study of absorbed fatty acids is performed on a sample of Kalinga cooking pots and several types of foods. Pots used to cook vegetables and meat could be discriminated from rice cooking pots. Except for rice, it was difficult to identify individual plant or animal species based on the absorbed fatty acids, although in several cases it could be determined that the pots were used to cook meat. A sample of Kalinga sherds, excavated from a midden, were also analyzed to explore fatty acid preservation in a depositional environment. It was found that two processes, oxidation and hydrolysis, either destroyed or altered the fatty acids to a point that made identification impossible. An appraisal is made of the current state of fatty acid research and how archaeologists can now employ this form of analysis in their ceramic studies.

Chapter 6 explores surface attrition and pottery use, which is analogous to much of the lithic use-wear research. Nine areas on the interior and exterior of Kalinga cooking vessels are found to have surface attrition that reflect use. A discussion of use activities that created these patterns is offered, and an assessment is made of the activities that are not recorded as traces on the pottery surface. It is found that vegetable/meat and rice cooking pots have very similar exterior attrition but that four areas on the interior of the vessels are modified in very different ways. Use traces on these four interior areas reflect different activities associated with vegetable/meat and rice cooking. In this chapter, the general process of ceramic attrition is explored so that similar analyses can now be performed on prehistoric pottery assemblages.

Carbon deposition on pottery surfaces is the topic of Chapter 7. Interior carbon deposition results from the charring of food and is governed by several factors: source of heat, intensity of heat, and presence of moisture. In the Kalinga pottery sample, interior carbon deposition reflects both what was cooked and how it was heated. Exterior carbon deposition, or soot, was also investigated. The soot on Kalinga cooking pots is described and matched to actual cooking activity. The processes of soot deposition, governed by wood type, temperature of the ceramic surface, and the presence of moisture, are initially found to be unclear.

Several experiments are performed on previously unused Kalinga pottery and on replicated ceramic pieces to explore soot deposition in greater detail. Based on these data, archaeologists should now be able to make specific inferences about how pottery was positioned over a fire and some general activities of use based only upon soot that now adheres to the exterior of their pots.

Some concluding thoughts are provided in Chapter 8. The research is reviewed briefly, and the importance of a combined experimental and ethnoarchaeological approach is emphasized. A final assessment is also made of the three forms of pottery use alteration (residues, carbon deposits, and surface attrition). It is argued that by combining these three analytical strategies, archaeologists can begin to make accurate assessments of how pottery was used in the past.

Chapter **2**

Ethnoarchaeology and Experimental Archaeology Defined

Ethnoarchaeology and experimental archaeology have become established subfields in archaeology; so much so that it is possible to be an archaeologist but spend little time excavating or analyzing materials from an archaeological site. During the inception of the modern era of ethnoarchaeology and experimental archaeology, which I place at the beginning of the "new archaeology," there was an abundance of theoretical statements and attempts at defining the scope of these new subfields (see the papers in Donnan and Clewlow 1974a). Not since the work of Reid *et al.* (1975) and Tringham (1978), however, has there been a discussion, from a theoretical perspective, of what comprises ethnoarchaeology and experimental archaeology and how they interrelate. There is certainly a need, especially in experimental archaeology, for a refinement of definitions and a discussion of how each subfield relates to the primary objective of archaeology—understanding the relationships between human behavior and material objects. From the perspective of having participated in both ethnoarchaeology and experimental archaeology, I provide working definitions of each subfield. I argue that ethnoarchaeology and experimental archaeology pursue the same archaeological objective (see Reid *et al.* 1975) but that they can be contrasted by the manner in which they control variables and the data each subfield analyzes. I also argue that combining ethnoarchaeology and experimental archaeology has the greatest potential for examining issues of archaeological importance. A case study is used to demonstrate this strategy and the insights it can provide.

ETHNOARCHAEOLOGY DEFINED

Jesse W. Fewkes is given credit for coining the term *ethnoarchaeologist* (Longacre 1991a:1; Oswalt 1974; Stanislawski 1974). Fewkes (1900:578-579) referred to himself as an "ethno-archaeologist" while gathering information among the Hopi in order to trace the migrational history of contemporary clans. Because Fewkes recognized a continuity between prehistoric and historic groups in this area, he utilized ethnographic data to help solve archaeological questions. This work and other contemporary archaeological investigations (e.g., Cushing 1886; Mindeleff 1896) reflect an evolutionary theoretical framework that dominated anthropological theory at that time. Prehistoric sites affiliated with contemporary ethnographic groups were seen as logical places to trace the evolutionary trajectories of various cultural and material traits. The ethnographic record played an important role in much of this early archaeological work. The following era in archaeological method and theory, referred to as the "classificatory-historical period" (Willey and Sabloff 1980), witnessed a decreased importance of ethnographic material. The concern was with placing cultural elements recovered archaeologically into the correct historical arrangement. This form of prehistoric research had little use for the ethnographic record.

Though a number of scholars during this period did not agree with this restrictive focus of archaeology (e.g., Bennett 1943; Martin 1938:297; Steward and Setzler 1938), the impetus for change was provided by the now-famous reviews of archaeology by Kluckhohn (1940) and Taylor (1983 [originally published, 1948]). Kluckhohn (1940:42) believed that archaeologists were involved in "a great deal of obsessive wallowing in detail of and for itself." Taylor (1983) shared this view of then-contemporary archaeology and offered an approach that included an increased usage of ethnographic materials. In constructing what he called the "cultural context," he suggested that archaeologists rely heavily on ethnographic data (Taylor 1983:170-172). Though the impact of Taylor's work was not immediate (Watson 1983:x), it had a significant and lasting impact on archaeology and in the way ethnographic data can be used in making inferences about the past.

Several works in particular demonstrated a renewed interest in ethnographic data. Thompson (1958) was the first archaeologist in several decades to perform a prolonged and detailed investigation of a living community. This work was done to explore the inferential process in archaeology, which—according to many—is dependent upon ethnographic analogy. Thompson (1958:149-150) states that "no progress can be made without the continued accumulation of adequate ethnographic information," although he maintains that cultural anthropologists will be the primary source for analogs in the inferential process (cf. Thompson 1991). Kleindienst and Watson (1956), in contrast, see both museum collections and ethnographies as inadequate sources for analogies. They recommend that the archaeologist "take to the field of living communities with . . . [their] own theoretical orientation and gather the necessary information in . . . [their] own way" (Kleindienst and Watson 1956:77).

Chang (1958) demonstrated how the ethnographic record can be systematically implemented to make inferences about the past. His task was to look at correlations between dwelling site and social grouping and then test the correlation with prehistoric material. The lasting impact of Chang's work, however, was that he was beginning to develop the means whereby ethnographic data can be used in archaeological interpretation. This set the stage for the "new archaeology" and what is the modern era of ethnoarchaeological research. At this point in archaeological history, several common features emerged as researchers became increasingly dissatisfied with traditional archaeological work: (1) there was a growing consensus about the need for explanation; (2) culture, including technology, was seen as a system with functional relationships to both the social and natural environment; and (3) the ethnographic record was considered to be an important source for analogical arguments. What was lacking, however, was the means to use appropriately gathered ethnographic data in archaeological explanation. Primarily through the work of Binford and his colleagues, it was shown how ethnographic data can be employed in archaeological explanation that goes beyond simple analogical arguments.

Binford (1968:13) notes that "increased ethnographic knowledge cannot by themselves increase our knowledge of the past." He introduces a new methodology that "demands the rigorous testing of deductively drawn hypotheses against independent sets of data" (Binford 1968:13). The ethnographic record, in this framework, serves as the source of such hypotheses, and the work of each of the first "new archaeologists" (e.g., Deetz 1965; Hill 1970; Longacre 1970) employs the ethnographic record in this way.

Although the present discussion has been an overly simplistic and North American-centered review of the use of ethnographic data in archaeological inference, it should at least demonstrate the common thread that links previous work with contemporary ethnoarchaeological research. I refer to the period since the "new archaeology" as the current era in ethnoarchaeology because it puts a new emphasis on ethnographic data that continues to the present.

This new emphasis in archaeology had two outcomes. First, there was an evaluation of the appropriateness of various forms of ethnographic data in archaeological interpretation, and a debate, continuing to the present, about how ethnographic analogy should be used in reconstructions of prehistory (e.g., Binford 1984a,b, 1985, 1987; Gould 1985; Gould and Watson 1982; Murray and Walker 1988; Wylie 1982, 1985). Second, archaeologists began collecting their own ethnographic data (e.g., Binford 1978; David and Hennig 1972; Gould 1971; Longacre 1974; Pastron 1974; Yellen 1977). It was found that ethnographies often lacked information useful to the archaeologist. Consequently, many archaeologists are presently involved in collecting or at least using ethnographic data. Although this research is commendable and has raised the level of archaeological inference, it has also created a good deal of confusion about what ethnoarchaeology really is.

Those who have examined the history of ethnoarchaeological research probably share the frustration of trying to compose a definition of a subfield that has consisted of archaeologists doing ethnographic fieldwork, but also historical archaeology or merely the use of ethnographic data in archaeological inference. For the purpose of discussion, I will divide the myriad uses of ethnoarchaeology into two categories: ethnoarchaeology as everything and ethnoarchaeology: a more restrictive usage.

Ethnoarchaeology as Everything

Donnan and Clewlow (1974b:i), in the preface for one of the first edited monographs on ethnoarchaeology, stated that this subfield of anthropology "is relatively new and should therefore be loosely defined." That was an acceptable strategy as the field searched for an identity, but today ethnoarchaeology must be clearly defined or risk becoming a meaningless term (Kent 1987:33). Although much of the research called "ethnoarchaeology" has been productive, it is such an amalgam that archaeology is now at the point of either dropping the term, because currently it leads to confusion instead of understanding, or forming a consensus about what ethnoarchaeology really is. I prefer the latter course. Therefore, I would argue against the all-inclusive use of ethnoarchaeology and what I call "ethnoarchaeology as everything."

This form of ethnoarchaeology is "defined broadly as encompassing all the theoretical and methodological aspects of comparing ethnographic and archaeological data" (Stiles 1977:87). Archaeologists, according to this view, are doing ethnoarchaeology if they employ any of the following information: ethnographic literature or material such as travel accounts or any archival data, experimental studies (also discussed later), museum collections, ethnographic analogy, archaeological ethnography (which can include the archaeologist's own use of material culture), or informant interviews. Consequently, some historical archaeologists have referred to their work as "ethnoarchaeology" because they employ archival data and informant interviews (e.g., Adams 1973; Brown 1973; James and Lindsay 1973; Oswalt and VanStone 1967; Staski 1991). One could more accurately call it ethnohistory or, in some cases, simply good historical archaeology in the sense that all relevant sources of information are employed.

But the broader question is, can ethnoarchaeology as defined here be distinguished from other aspects of archaeology? Ethnoarchaeology, defined so inclusively, encompasses many other aspects of contemporary American archaeology. Even the most simple inferences in archaeology, like the distinction between the use of jars and bowls in the American Southwest, are dependent upon ethnographic information. We are left, therefore, with the meaningless conclusion that all of archaeology is ethnoarchaeology.

Kent (1987) has tried to reduce the confusion about ethnoarchaeology but unfortunately has done the opposite. In her framework, "the goals of ethnoarchaeology are to formulate and test archaeologically oriented and/or derived methods, hypotheses, models, and theories with ethnographic data" (Kent 1987:37). It is a process that includes an archaeological problem, testing with ethnographic data, and application of the findings to archaeological data. This is the least acceptable definition of ethnoarchaeology because many of the most informative ethnoarchaeological research projects (e.g., DeBoer and Lathrap 1979; Kramer 1982; Longacre 1974, 1981) are not considered "ethnoarchaeology" by

Kent. I recommend that archaeology not use this or any of the all-inclusive definitions for ethnoarchaeology but instead employ a more restrictive usage favored by a good number of researchers involved in ethnoarchaeological research.

Ethnoarchaeology: A More Restrictive Usage

Ethnoarchaeology should be limited to archaeologists doing ethnographic fieldwork for the purpose of addressing archaeological questions. A number of researchers share this basic definition (e.g., Kramer 1982:1, 1985:77-78; Longacre 1981:50, 1991a; Schiffer 1978:230; Stanislawski 1974:15; Tringham 1978:170). In the discussion that follows, a number of points are taken from these and other researchers to develop a restricted definition of ethnoarchaeology.

First, the research should be conducted *by an archaeologist* (Longacre 1991a:1; cf. Thompson 1991:234). Some research that focuses on material culture or on behaviors related to material culture (e.g., Foster 1960; Reynolds and Scott 1987; Richardson 1974) can be of use in archaeology, but only the archaeologists, armed with a strategy for researching the ethnographic present unique to our field, will record the types of data necessary to address questions in archaeology. The initial call for "action archaeology" (Kleindienst and Watson 1956) resulted, in part, because the traditional ethnographies lacked information needed in archaeological inference. As Yellen (1977:xi) notes, the types of information that archaeologists need from studies of contemporary people, like a detailed map of where people throw each piece of bone and broken pot, are not found in ethnographies, nor should we expect them to be.

Second, ethnoarchaeological research *can take place among any extant people*. Although Stanislawski (1974:15) states that ethnoarchaeology should be done among nonindustrial groups, this restriction is unnecessarily limiting. Research among the last remaining hunter-gatherers or household pottery producers can provide insights, but some principles involved in the relationships between material culture and human behavior or the processes involved in the transformation of artifacts from systemic to archaeological context can be examined among people at any time or place (e.g., Gould and Schiffer 1981; Wilson *et al.* 1991).

Third, ethnoarchaeological research should *focus on archaeologically motivated questions* (Thompson 1991:231). In its most general sense, this refers to (1) the investigation of relationships between material culture and human behavior and organization (e.g., Arnold 1985; DeBoer and Lathrap 1979; Gould 1980; Graves 1985; Hayden and Cannon 1984; Kramer 1982; Longacre 1981; Longacre *et al.* 1988; Watson 1979), or the symbolic meaning of material items (e.g., Hodder 1982); and (2) researching the processes involved in the formation of an archaeological site (e.g., Binford 1978, 1981; Deal 1983, 1985; Hayden and Cannon 1983; Longacre 1985; Schiffer 1987; Yellen 1977). This does not mean, however, that ethnoarchaeologists must concern themselves only with issues of archaeology; there are problems of broader anthropological importance, such as the causes and consequences of population change (Kramer 1982:1) or issues of contemporary public policy (Rathje and Schiffer 1982:382-386) that can be addressed with ethnoarchaeological data.

Finally, the *ultimate objective of ethnoarchaeology should be to help understand the past.* Archaeology is the study of the relationships between material culture and human behavior and organization at any time or place (Reid *et al.* 1975; Schiffer 1976:4-9). Ethnoarchaeology as defined here, however, should be restricted to research among extant peoples for the purpose of addressing questions applicable to reconstructions of prehistory. In the strategies of behavioral archaeology proposed by Reid *et al.* (1975), ethnoarchaeology is confined to strategy 2. That is, ethnoarchaeology "pursues general questions in present material culture in order to acquire laws useful for the study of the past" (Reid *et al.* 1975:865). Certainly there are other forms of research among extant people that focus on material culture in order to explain and describe present behavior (e.g., Rathje 1990), but for the purpose of clarification I suggest that it not be called ethnoarchaeology.

The restricted definition of ethnoarchaeology gives this subfield a specific role in archaeology, unlike the diffuse and virtually useless definition given earlier. As a field develops, there is a need to refine our terms to promote better communication among scholars and to assist future research. This does not mean that the borders of ethnoarchaeological research are or should be rigid. Even in the most restricted definition of ethnoarchaeology, as given here, the borders with other subfields, like historical archaeology and especially experimental archaeology, can become indistinct (Schiffer 1978:230).

EXPERIMENTAL ARCHAEOLOGY DEFINED

Experimental archaeology is the fabrication of materials, behaviors, or both, in order to observe one or more processes involved in the production, use, discard, deterioration, or recovery of material culture. It is theoretically identical to ethnoarchaeology (Schiffer 1978:230; Tringham 1978:170) because both subfields focus on the interface between material culture, on the one hand, and human behavior, organization, meaning, and environment, on the other. Moreover, both ethnoarchaeology and experimental archaeology have the same objective: understanding the past by addressing questions with modern-day material culture (Reid *et al.* 1975:865). It should be noted that I am only referring to "experimental archaeology" and not "experiments in archaeology." The former consists of exploring relationships between material culture, human behavior, and the environment, and the latter consists of experiments performed to test the accuracy and reliability of archaeological recovery and analytical techniques (e.g., de Barros 1982; Fish 1978; Hodson 1970).

The history of experiments in archaeology mirrors ethnoarchaeology in that there was an initial interest around the turn of the century, a period of few experiments during the "classificatory-historical period" in American archaeology, and then a renewed interest in experimentation by 1950 and into the era of "new archaeology." Much of the earliest experimentation was with stone tools, and Johnson (1978:337-346) finds that this period was concerned primarily with determining whether stone objects were fashioned by humans or, in a rudimentary fashion, understand how ancient artifacts were used. Moreover, like the earliest ethnoarchaeological work, experiments were often conducted as a source of data for evolutionary explanations. For example, Cushing (1894) combined his knowledge of Zuni metallurgy with experiments to determine that copper artifacts found in the northeastern United States could have been worked with simple tools and methods available to the native inhabitants. This countered the popular notion at that time that the copper artifacts were not manufactured by members of the indigenous groups because the technology seemed too advanced.

Analogy of any sort, whether by ethnology or experiment, was not employed often during the subsequent period in American archaeology. Johnson (1978:343-449) finds that there was a dearth of experimentation with stone tools during the "classificatory-historical period" (Willey and

Sabloff 1980) and that the majority of experiments were not performed by professionally trained archaeologists.

Experimentation, like ethnoarchaeology, makes a comeback when archaeologists begin to be dissatisfied with mere classification and description. In fact, some of the same individuals that advocated a renewed interest in ethnography for explanation in archaeology also saw the importance of determining how artifacts were used. Steward and Setzler (1938:8) state that "archaeological objects would be more meaningful if they were regarded not simply as museum specimens but as tools employed by human beings." Taylor (1983:170) mirrors these sentiments and adds that "use, of whatever sort, probably has left some signs upon the artifact, e.g., scratches, smoothed areas, beveled edges." This marks a renewed interest in experimental archaeology but only in the sense of providing possibilities for how artifacts were used. Because experiments were considered just another form of analogy, it is not until the "new archaeology" that experiments or ethnographic data were integrated rigorously into archaeological explanation (a further discussion of analogy in archaeology is provided later).

Reviews of archaeological experiments can be found in Coles (1973, 1979) and Johnson (1978), and bibliographic lists of experiments have been compiled (e.g., Hester and Heizer 1973). In this section I do not provide another review of experiments in archaeology, but rather I discuss, on a general level, the role of experiments in archaeology. It is argued that the greatest challenge in experimental archaeology is to provide low-level principles, about the material-behavioral interface, that are readily usable in archaeological inference. Building on the work of Tringham (1978), a revised categorization of experiments is suggested that includes a strategy for devising such low-level principles.

Works by Ascher (1961a), Coles (1979), and Tringham (1978), each trying to introduce more scientific rigor into experimental archaeology, discuss the role of experiments in archaeological inference (see also Claassen 1981; Reid *et al.* 1975). Ascher (1961a:795) was referring to what he called "imitative experiments," which was an exercise that tested a "belief about what happened in the past." The imitative experiment was based on the assumption that cultural behavior is patterned and that artifacts used or produced in the same way today can reflect past cultural behavior (Ascher 1961a:802-807). He suggested a program to follow when conducting an experiment to increase confidence in the experimenter's results.

Coles (1979:46-48) offers an expanded regime for experiments in archaeology that includes selecting the appropriate materials and methods, repetition of the experiments, an "honest" evaluation of the experimental procedures, but most importantly an awareness that experimental results can never be taken as proof that something was made or used in a particular fashion. This "leap of faith" from experimental result to an inference regarding past behavior is a long-standing problem (e.g., Ascher 1961a:811-812), and it mirrors the concern with the appropriate use of ethnographic analogy.

Tringham (1978) deals with this issue, in part, by suggesting that there are two types of experiments: experiments on the "by-products of human behavior" and "behavioral experimentation." According to Tringham (1978:180), experiments in each category have "a different potential degree of confirmability inherent in its results: therefore different levels of inference and different kinds of interpretation are appropriate to each."

Experiments on the by-products of human behavior are intended to reconstruct the human and natural agents of artifact modification such as wear, damage, or decay. Tringham includes her own work with lithic use-wear in this category (Tringham *et al.* 1974) along with other lithic use-wear analyses. Other research that fits roughly in this category includes more recent lithic use-wear studies (e.g., Hayden 1979; Keeley 1980; Vaughn 1985), portions of ceramic experiments (e.g., Bronitsky and Hamer 1986; Mabry *et al.* 1988; Skibo and Schiffer 1987; Vaz Pinto *et al.* 1987), and research designed to explore the natural processes of artifact modification (e.g., Bowers *et al.* 1983; Jewell and Dimbleby 1966; Skibo 1987; Villa and Courtin 1983).

Behavioral experimentation is "the more risky testing of upper-level propositions about activities of which there is no direct archaeological evidence" (Tringham 1978:182). Tringham (1978:183) notes that most experiments performed, referred to as "imitative" by Ascher (1961a), are considered part of this category. She believes that experiments on the by-products of human behavior are quantifiable, repeatable, and more "sciencelike" because they conform to natural laws. Behavioral experiments, in contrast, are nonquantifiable and difficult to test because human variables are involved.

Although I concur generally with Tringham's approach to experimental archaeology, I cannot adopt it fully. Recently there has been a great increase in the number of experiments in archaeology, and few fit completely into either category. As a group, the only experiments that fit neatly into "by-product tests" are those that study artifact modification by natural processes (e.g., Bowers *et al.* 1983; Skibo 1987) or the basic principles in lithic fracture mechanics (Speth 1974) or ceramic strength (Mabry *et al.* 1988; Vaz Pinto *et al.* 1987). The majority of both lithic and ceramic experiments combines elements of each of Tringham's categories. For example, Skibo *et al.* (1989a; see also Lewenstein 1987) explore many of the primary relationships between technology and pottery use properties but also apply these findings to an archaeological problem in areas that Tringham (1978) would refer to as "behavioral experimentation."

If one believes that a major objective of experimental archaeology (and ethnoarchaeology) is generating material-behavioral correlates, then the dichotomy that Tringham proposes dissolves. Though Tringham is correct in noting that there are many levels of experimentation, the results that are provided are correlates, and all are used similarly in archaeological inference. This may be just a simple reformulation of Tringham's (1978) concepts, but I think that the distinction is important. The relationship between temper size and heating effectiveness of pottery is a material-behavioral correlate as is the relationship between residential mobility and house type. Although they are at different levels of abstraction, each correlate is used in a similar fashion, when combined with other information, to make inferences about the past. One important task for the experimental archaeologist (along with the ethnoarchaeologist) is to provide correlates that can be readily applied to archaeological inference. This is done by an approach that, ideally, begins with controlled laboratory experiments and concludes with observations in situations with far less control over the variables involved. For the purpose of illustration, experimental studies will be discussed as either "controlled laboratory experiments" or "field experiments."

Controlled Laboratory Experiments

Experiments in this category involve a high degree of control of the variables. A primary feature of controlled laboratory experiments is replicability. Researchers anywhere should be able to acquire the same materials, perform the experiment, and attain identical results. Ideally, all variables but one are held constant. Examples of controlled laboratory experiments include Bronitsky and Hamer's (1986) investigation of the effects of temper on thermal shock resistance and Young and Stone's (1990) study of the thermal properties of textured ceramics. This category is different than Tringham's "by-products" experimentation because it does not preclude the possibility of exploring how the low-level principles relate to behavioral elements such as individual choice and how they affect technological change (see Schiffer and Skibo 1987).

The result of a controlled laboratory experiment should be in the form of general principles that explain or describe the relationship between a technological property of a material item and some behaviorally meaningful unit. In some ceramic experiments, for example, principles have been generated that describe the relationship between temper and various pottery performance characteristics, such as heating effectiveness, thermal shock, and workability (Skibo *et al.* 1989a). Some have failed to understand the importance of these low-level principles, even referring to them as "Mickey Mouse laws" (Flannery 1973:51), but they are the foundation of all archaeological inference (cf. Salmon 1982). One reason for the misunderstanding regarding the importance of these low-level principles is that they appear far too removed from an archaeological inference of the past. But one cannot take a single principle generated in a controlled laboratory experiment and immediately proceed to make inferences about the past. One low-level principle, or correlate, must be combined with other such principles and many other sources of information, including higher level theory, before the archaeologist can proceed to reliable inferences (cf. Schiffer 1988a).

Ideally, it is best to explore a single material-behavioral correlate at various levels. For example, under controlled laboratory conditions it can be determined that temper size affects heating effectiveness of pottery. But, to make this correlation more readily usable in archaeological inference, it would be important to look at the relationship between temper size and heating effectiveness under more behaviorally relevant, less controlled, conditions. So one might look at this relationship under more natural conditions such as by using openfiring and traditional forming techniques—these are "field experiments."

Field Experiments

In this category, experimenters give up some control of the variables, imposed in the previous stage, to test hypotheses under more natural (i.e., behaviorally relevant) conditions. Examples of field experiments would include investigating the efficiency of replicated stone tools for butchering (e.g., Huckell 1979, 1982), having contemporary Mayans use replicated stone tools (Lewenstein 1987), or making and firing pottery using local clays and natural conditions (e.g., Vitelli 1984).

The results of field experiments, like controlled laboratory experiments, are in the form of low-level principles but at a much less abstract level. Field experiments serve the purpose of filling out a particular material-behavioral correlate by exploring how other elements factor into the relationship. Ideally, addressing a particular archaeological problem should proceed first through the controlled laboratory stage, to investigate the processes involved, and then to the field stage. For example, in the investigation of how pottery surface treatments affect water permeability (e.g., Schiffer 1988b), it is best to start in the controlled laboratory stage. One would hold constant all ceramic variability (e.g., temper, clay type, firing temperature) except surface treatment. Using standard briquettes or even miniature vessels the effect of surface treatments on water permeability could be tested. Based on these findings, the experimenter could then proceed to test how other sources of variability, like temper or firing temperature, influence water permeability and especially how they may work in concert with surface treatment to affect this relationship. The objective at this point would be to introduce more natural conditions into the experiment. In this hypothetical example, the results of these tests may lead the experimenter to make an inference about a particular case of pottery variability and change. In the most ideal situation, the researcher could also explore this issue ethnoarchaeologically and begin to understand some of the nontechnofunctional factors involved in the application of a surface treatment.

ETHNOARCHAEOLOGY AND EXPERIMENTAL ARCHAEOLOGY

In this final section I will discuss the shared characteristics of ethnoarchaeology and experimental archaeology, the nature of each subfield's data and how experimental archaeology and ethnoarchaeology can be combined to address issues of archaeological importance.

As was noted, there still remains a good deal of confusion about what comprises both ethnoarchaeology and experimental archaeology. In the most extreme examples, Dillon (1984:2) believes that experimental archaeology is part of ethnoarchaeology, whereas others (e.g., Ingersoll *et al.* 1977) maintain that research such as replication experiments, studies of site formation, and ethnoarchaeology should all be considered under the rubric of experimental archaeology. Both subfields do share common objectives, but a number of differences make research in each area distinct. Obviously there is a difference in the amount that variables of interest can be controlled. But also, ethnoarchaeology and experimental archaeology differ in the types of information that can be gathered. In the following section I discuss research in each subfield and argue that combining ethnoarchaeology and experimental archaeology can be a fruitful strategy for developing material-behavioral correlates that are more readily applied in archaeological inference.

Ethnoarchaeological and Experimental Research

Although ethnoarchaeology and experimental archaeology have common objectives, there is a difference in the type of data that can be obtained. In the most general sense, if the objective is to generate material-behavioral correlates, the experimental archaeologist is confined most often to the material side of the equation, whereas the strength of ethnoarchaeology lies in the ability to observe behavior directly. Two areas of investigation, in particular, have been pursued in both subfields: the study of formation processes and artifact function.

The study of cultural and, particularly, noncultural formation processes, is well suited to experimental investigation. A number of studies (e.g., Bowers *et al.* 1983; Lancaster 1986) have replicated various processes of site formation and generated lawlike statements that can be applied in archaeological inference. Some ethnoarchaeological research (e.g., Binford 1978; Deal 1985; DeBoer and Lathrap 1979; Hayden and Cannon 1983) has also focused on various site formation processes.

Another important area of research in both subfields is artifact function (i.e., techno-, ideo-, and sociofunction). Chapter 3 provides a more complete discussion of function, but it is sufficient to say here that all artifacts can possess techno-, ideo-, and sociofunctions. The experimental archaeologist, however, is most often limited to the investigation of technofunction. Such research includes studying how things were made, how things were used, and how the maker and user of the item altered the shape, form, or composition to adjust to changing environmental conditions. A number of lithic and ceramic studies have investigated some aspect of technofunction (e.g., Bronitsky and Hamer 1986; Odell and Cowan 1986; Salls 1985; Skibo et al. 1989a). But it must be remembered that technofunction is just one of three functional sources of artifact variability.

Ethnoarchaeological research, in contrast, is not so limited. Ethnoarchaeology can explore beyond technofunction into the areas of artifact socio- and ideofunction. A number of ethnoarchaeological studies have explored how nontechnofunctional factors affect the manufacture and use of material items (e.g., Aronson et al. n.d.; Arnold 1983; Graves 1985; Hodder 1982; Longacre 1981). Moreover, ethnoarchaeology can also develop material-behavioral or material-organizational correlates at higher levels of abstraction. Examples of such research include demonstrating correlations between architecture and household size (e.g., Hayden and Cannon 1984; Kramer 1979), investigating the relationship between material items and wealth (e.g., Hayden and Cannon 1984; Trostel n.d.), and studying the factors involved in the production and distribution of pottery (Allen 1984; Nicklin 1981; Stark n.d., 1991).

Generating Material-Behavioral Correlates

In ethnoarchaeology and experimental archaeology, there are two related issues that must be considered when generating material-behavioral correlates. The first is the issue of behavioral significance and the second is putting the material-behavioral correlate, or any results, into a form that is readily usable in archaeological inference. It is important, however, to introduce first the issue of ethnographic analogy.

The modern debate over ethnographic analogy dates back to the works of Ascher (1961b) and Thompson (1956), with the most recent discussions involving Binford (1984a, 1985, 1987), Gould (1971, 1985; Gould and Watson 1982), Watson (1982), and Wylie (1982, 1985). Briefly, Binford (1967) maintains that ethnographic analogies should not be used to verify archaeological reconstructions; rather, analogies should serve as the source for gathering plausible hypotheses to be tested with archaeological data. More recently, Binford (1987) has rephrased the argument but has continued this line of reasoning. He contends that ethnographic analogies should serve as "frames of reference" against which the archaeologist can compare prehistoric material. Gould, in contrast, believes that the strict use of ethnographic analogy unnecessarily constrains how we perceive the archaeological record and prehistoric behavior (Gould and Watson 1982). Gould (1980) is primarily concerned with interpreting premodern human behavior, and thus he contends that modern analogs can be inappropriate. Wylie (1982) attempts to forge a middle ground by demonstrating that Gould's reasoning is in fact analogical (see also Watson 1982) and that analogy is unavoidable in archaeological inference.

Wylie (1985:105) suggests that "the strategies for improving analogical arguments suggested by the logic of analogy constitute mutually reinforcing procedures for checking the adequacy of both interpretive conclusions and interpretive assumptions about the uniformity, in particular aspects, of past and present." Murray and Walker (1988) build upon the work of Wylie and propose that archaeology should develop "archaeological performance criteria" for evaluating hypotheses derived from analogy and that one important criterion for analogies is that they must be potentially refutable with the archaeological data of interest.

The debate over the role of analogy in archaeological inference has been instructive, especially in elucidating the approaches of the various scholars. But if one accepts the definition of ethnoarchaeology and experimental archaeology as subfields of archaeology designed to generate correlations between material items and human behavior, analogy is of little importance. An archaeological inference is a descriptive statement about past cultural behavior or organization that is developed from material-behavioral (or material-organizational) correlates, and principles that describe cultural and noncultural formation processes (Schiffer 1972, 1975). The results of experimental archaeology and ethnoarchaeology are used to develop low-level principles in these areas. Ethnographic analogy as described does not have a central role.

The primary problem in ethnoarchaeological and experimental research is formulating material-behavioral correlates in such a way that will be useful in archaeological inference (cf. Schiffer 1981:905). It could be said that this is just another way to describe analogical arguments, but there is a fundamental difference. The objective of ethnoarchaeology and experimental archaeology is to develop low-level principles to be tested against the archaeological record. Research should focus on putting ethnoarchaeological and experimental results into a form that is more readily applied in archaeological inference. Two examples are used to illustrate this point.

It was demonstrated (Skibo *et al.* 1989b) that in the study of ceramic style, results obtained in ethnoarchaeology are rarely applied in prehistoric ceramic analysis because there is a disjunction between units of analysis and observation (see also Reid 1973). Ethnoarchaeologists, with some exceptions, develop their models based on whole pots and do not use analytical units applicable in archaeological inference. Moreover, analytic units in the analysis of prehistoric ceramics are most often sherds, making concordance difficult between models in ethnoarchaeology and archaeological inference. The solution in both areas of study is to concentrate on the processes that transform whole vessels into sherds.

The second example deals with the problems involved in using experimental results, which can be different than those encountered with ethnoarchaeological data. Experimental studies have the advantage of control of their variables but must deal with problems of behavioral significance (see Schiffer and Skibo 1987).

When conducting an experiment with laboratory controls, one is likely to find positive relationships. For example, a heavily tempered pot has less overall strength than a comparable vessel with less temper. If one were to make ceramic tiles of compositions identical to these vessels and perform a strength test, one would doubtless find statistically significant differences in strength. The important question is, however, would the pottery users be aware of this difference in strength, that is, is strength in this case behaviorally significant, and under what conditions do people act on perceived differences in performance characteristics like strength? Not all differences, even statistically significant differences, are *behaviorally* significant. The archaeologist must determine behavioral significance based, usually, on ethnoarchaeological or ethnographic information.

Another component of behavioral significance is equifinality. If the experimenter finds that a ceramic surface treatment decreases permeability, does that imply that the prehistoric potter altered the surface for this reason? The answer is "not necessarily." In the particular case of pottery, any technical choice affects many performance characteristics. For example, large temper may increase thermal shock resistance, abrasion resistance, and any number of manufacturing performance characteristics (Skibo *et al.* 1989a). Because of the multiple effects of any one particular technical choice, the potter or pottery user must make compromises in various performance characteristics. The experimental archaeologist must look at technological properties in this broad framework. One must rely on ethnoarchaeological and ethnographic data to understand technical choices and how they change.

Therefore, the important issue is not if an analogy is appropriate but whether the low-level principles developed in ethnoarchaeology and experimental archaeology can be readily applied in archaeological inference. Ethnoarchaeologists must build their models based on the same analytic units used with prehistoric material (e.g., Deal 1983), and the experimental archaeologist must grapple with the issue of behavioral significance. For ethnoarchaeologists and experimental archaeologists to reach this new level requires exploring at various levels any one correlate or formation process principle. The data generated by ethnoarchaeological or experimental research are more applicable to archaeological inference if the investigation is undertaken in both a tightly controlled environment and in situations with more natural conditions. The following example (see also Lewenstein 1987) demonstrates this by combining controlled laboratory experiments, field experiments, and ethnoarchaeological research to investigate a single material-behavioral correlate.

Case Study

In a series of controlled laboratory experiments, Skibo *et al.* (1989a) proposed that heating effectiveness and a number of other performance characteristics would be important to people under certain cooking conditions. This was done in the context of trying to determine what performance characteristics were important in the transition from the Late Archaic fiber-tempered pottery to the Early Woodland sand-tempered ceramics. The conclusions reached in this study were based on the assumption that people would be aware of certain performance characteristics particularly in the context of ceramic change. But inferences that rely heavily on controlled laboratory experiments often leave important questions unanswered. First, under which specific conditions do people become aware of the performance characteristics of pottery, and second, which nontechnofunctional performance characteristics are important in such a relationship? Only focused ethnoarchaeological work and field experiments can begin to address these questions.

As part of the pottery use-alteration research, I collected data and performed field experiments relevant to these issues (Skibo n.d.). Kalinga households are in the process of replacing traditional ceramic cooking vessels with metal pots. Although nearly every household has enough metal pots for all of their cooking, only rice cooking is done consistently with the metal containers; vegetable and meat cooking is still done primarily with ceramic pots. The Kalinga women state that they use metal pots for cooking rice because it cooks faster (heating effectiveness). A field experiment found that the metal vessels reached the boiling point between 1 and 5 minutes faster than comparable ceramic vessels. When asked why they did not use metal pots for cooking vegetables and meat, they stated that (1) the metal pots cooked too fast, often boiling over, whereas the ceramic pots would simmer without boiling over; and (2) that the metal pots were too difficult to wash.

The metal pots are difficult to wash because the Kalinga insist on making the vessels shiny by removing all of the exterior soot. This requires laborious scrubbing with sand and water because some of the soot has actually penetrated the metal surface; metal pots take more than twice as long to wash as do comparable ceramic vessels (Skibo n.d.). Black soot adhering to the exterior surface of metal pots does not affect cooking performance, but it does influence the appearance of the vessels. Shiny pots are preferred because they are hung by their handles individually in their houses (ceramic pots in contrast may be put in the rafters or stacked on shelves). Metal vessels can cost up to 10 times more than comparable ceramic vessels, and the ability to buy them is related to household wealth (Trostel n.d.). Apparently, metal pots also serve as a sign of modernization, wealth, and overall economic position.

A number of important findings were made in this case study (see also Aronson *et al.* n.d.). The ethnoarchaeological research demonstrated that a performance characteristic, in this case heating effectiveness (a concept first explored under controlled laboratory conditions), is important to Kalinga cooks. A field experiment demonstrated that the differences they perceived in heating effectiveness between metal and ceramic vessels is only several minutes. Moreover, the ethnoarchaeological study illustrated that a performance characteristic like heating effectiveness is important to the pottery users, particularly in the context of technological change.

The ethnoarchaeological work also permitted the exploration of nontechnofunctional performance characteristics that are important in technological change. Although it was found that heating effectiveness was the most important factor in both the adoption of metal vessels for cooking rice and the retention of ceramic pots for cooking vegetables and meat, a nontechnofunctional performance characteristic was shown to play a secondary role in the continued use of ceramic vessels. Ease of washing, a nontechnofunctional performance characteristic related to the display of the metal vessels, was found to be important in the retention of ceramic cooking vessels.

This case study underscores the great potential held by the combination of ethnoarchaeology and experimental archaeology for understanding the relationship between material culture and human behavior. When a focused ethnoarchaeological project is not possible, an attempt should be made to reduce some of the control of the variables, in the form of field experiments, to "flesh out" a particular material-behavioral correlate and make it more readily usable in archaeological inference. Ideally, the low-level principles developed in ethnoarchaeology and experimental archaeology would then be used to explain archaeological phenomena. The work by Sassaman (1991), on the development and distribution of Late Archaic pottery in the Southeast United States, provides an excellent example of how such principles can be integrated into archaeological inference.

Chapter *3*

Pottery Use Alteration

The previous chapter defined ethnoarchaeology and experimental archaeology and discussed their relationship to archaeological inference. This chapter outlines the role of pottery use-alteration studies in archaeology, focusing on how they can be employed to determine technofunction. Research of pottery technofunction focuses on two different components of pottery utilization: intended and actual use. Recent work in each area is reviewed, and it is argued that research that reconstructs how pottery was actually used, principally through use-alteration analysis, provides the best information for reconstructing past activity. The final section of the chapter outlines a framework for pottery use alteration. Drawing on lithic use-wear research, this framework incorporates all forms of ceramic alteration (use- and nonuse-related) from pottery manufacture through archaeological recovery.

POTTERY FUNCTION

Material objects possessed by people can be referred to as their technology, which comprises not only the artifacts but also the knowledge for creating and using them (Kingery 1989; Schiffer and Skibo 1987:595). Archaeologists traditionally divide material culture variability into stylistic or functional categories (e.g., Jelinek 1976). In this chapter, following Sackett (1977:370), the term *function* refers to more than an artifact's utilitarian role; the function of any single artifact is determined by how it performs in a society's technology—technofunction, sociofunction, and ideofunction (Rathje and Schiffer 1982:67-69; Schiffer n.d.; Schiffer and Skibo 1987:598-600). Technofunction refers to utilitarian aspects of an artifact's use, and socio- and ideofunctions are components of artifact variability traditionally placed within the stylistic category (cf. Binford 1962, 1965). All three, however, influence artifact design, and each must be considered when documenting and ultimately explaining technological variability and change.

A surface alteration study falls within the realm of technofunction, although a strategy for determining how an artifact was used can lead to a better understanding of socio- and ideofunctions (Plog 1980:18-19). Technofunctions, however, have a number of unique qualities. First, the majority of artifacts of concern to archaeologists are made to be used— fulfill some utilitarian or technofunction. A structure must stand up for a period of time and provide protection and shelter; the edge of a stone ax must be sharp to cut wood but still tough enough to withstand repeated blows; and a cooking pot must not break when put over a hot fire. That same cooking pot may serve sociofunctions, in that it may have morphological characteristics unique to a certain group of households or a region and therefore symbolize group membership, but it still must be able to perform as a cooking vessel at an acceptable level.

The second reason why technofunctions are unique is that they are closely related to subsistence and the overall settlement system. For example, vessels used in different activities can be designed to fit that activity with alterations in physical properties such as paste composition (Bronitsky 1986) or shape (Smith 1985). Moreover, changes in diet and cooking practices (Braun 1983; Skibo *et al.* 1989a) or settlement mobility (Skibo *et al.* 1989a) can affect vessel design.

Finally, archaeologists are now equipped to reconstruct technofunction. For example, observable and measurable properties such as vessel shape, size and density of temper, and surface treatment are often related to vessel technofunction (for a review, see Bronitsky 1986). This does not imply that sociofunction and ideofunction are less important, only that technofunctional relationships are more readily studied. At present, the most appropriate method for exploring the functions of a technology may be first to investigate and understand the technofunctional relationships before assigning socio- or ideofunctions. Indeed, making inferences about an artifact's sociofunction, for example, may be inappropriate if all factors related to artifact utility have not been explored.

Technofunction and methods to identify technofunction can be divided broadly into two groups: studies that reconstruct what an artifact was designed for—*intended* function—and research that investigates how the artifact was in fact used—*actual* function (see also Henrickson 1990; Rice 1987:207-242, 1990). In pottery analysis, both areas of inquiry are important; one can provide a framework of use activity, and the other can provide direct evidence of use (Griffiths 1978:69). One need only look at our own material culture to witness that intended and actual technofunction often are not identical; screwdrivers are used to pry open paint cans, and dining-room tables can be the place of numerous activities not related to food preparation and consumption such as writing dissertations or building model ships. In an ideal pottery analysis, information about both intended and actual vessel use would be provided because they are not mutually exclusive categories; each is necessary to reconstruct vessel technofunction.

Intended Vessel Technofunction

Ceramic vessels are better suited to a number of uses than baskets, gourds, or containers made of animal skin or wood (Rice 1987:208-210). Their primary advantages are that they can be placed over heat without being destroyed, and they can be used for long-term storage of liquids or dry goods, protecting their contents from moisture and vermin. Rice (1987:209) lists three broad categories of vessel use: storage, processing, and transfer. Including factors such as whether the contents are wet or dry, hot or cold, the duration of use and the distance of transfer, Rice breaks down these categories into 17 types of vessel use. Similarly, Smith (1988:913-914) in an examination of the ethnographic literature lists 14 use categories that include dry storage, long-term storage of dry materials, short-term storage of beverages or water, long-term storage of potables, storage of liquid nonpotables, general cooking, boiling, mechanical processing, eating, drinking, serving food, serving or pouring liquids, and long- or short-distance transport of potables.

Pottery, which is better than other containers for a number of uses, can be altered to better suit the intended technofunction. In manufacture, vessel properties such as morphology, paste composition, wall thickness, and surface treatment can be manipulated.

Morphological Properties and Technofunction

Archaeologists have a long-standing interest in the relationship between vessel size, shape, and use (for a review, see Rice 1987:211-226; Smith 1983). However, in much of southwestern archaeology, for example, such correlations do not often go beyond making the simple distinction between jars, thought to be used for cooking and storage, and bowls that are usually thought of as serving or eating vessels. These use designations, based implicitly on analogy with contemporary groups, are too general and lack sufficient theoretical and methodological rigor to be of much use for many research questions.

Other studies, however, have made more detailed inferences about pottery use from attributes of vessel size and shape (e.g., Braun 1980; Deal 1982; Hally 1986; Henrickson 1990; Howard 1981; Linton 1944; Lischka 1978; Nelson 1981). One profitable area of inquiry has focused on the development of uniformitarian predictors of use, based on ethnographic data, from vessel size and shape attributes (e.g., Henrickson and McDonald 1983; Smith 1983, 1985, 1988). Smith (1983) correlated categories of use to vessel attributes and found three that are the best predictors of use: relative openness of the vessel profile, rim diameter, and volume (Smith 1988:914; cf. Rice 1987:224-226). Research such as this is important because it has cross-cultural applicability and it is based upon measurements that are quantifiable and easily made on archaeological ceramics. A drawback is that one needs whole or nearly whole vessels to make the measurements, although there are means to gather shape and size data from sherds (e.g., Ericson and De Atley 1976; Plog 1985).

Physical Properties and Technofunction

Varying the shape and size of a pot is just one way the potter could create a vessel better suited to a particular use. There is considerable ethnographic (e.g., DeBoer and Lathrap 1979; Kramer 1985; Rogers 1936; Rye 1981; Thompson 1958) and experimental (Bronitsky and Hamer 1986; Skibo *et al.* 1989a; Steponaitis 1983; Tankersley and Meinhart 1982; Vaz Pinto *et al.* 1987) evidence that discrete physical properties of a vessel, easily manipulated by the potter, are related to vessel use. Moreover, physical properties are important during manufacture *and* use (Aronson *et al.* n.d.; Bronitsky 1986:212-220). These can be investigated by exploring behaviorally relevant performance characteristics (Schiffer and Skibo 1987). Some of the performance characteristics of manufacture include clay workability, paste shrinkage, changes during firing, and firing success. During use, important performance characteristics include thermal shock resistance, impact and abrasion resistance, heating effectiveness, and evaporative cooling effectiveness (Bronitsky 1986:212-218; Rice 1987:54-110, 226-232; Skibo *et al.* 1989a). One problem, from the potter's and pottery-user's perspective, is that alterations in physical properties can affect a number of performance characteristics. For example, organic temper may provide advantages in manufacture, but the product will be a less durable and efficient cooking pot than a comparable sand-tempered vessel (Skibo *et al.* 1989a).

Stimmell *et al.* (1982) provide an interesting example of how changes in one manufacturing performance characteristic require adjustments in others. They suggest that potters of the central United States during the prehistoric Mississippian period began making pots out of clay that was high in montmorillonite. The potters also began adding limestone or shell to make the montmorillonite clays more workable. However, shell decomposes during firing (usually between 600-900° C), and the subsequent uptake of water during and after cooling causes spalling or "limeblowing." Stimmell *et al.* (1982) suggest that to solve the problem the potters added salt, which reacts chemically with constituents of the paste and permits the vessels to be fired within the range of shell decomposition.

Many analytical techniques developed in materials science can provide new insights into pottery manufacture and use (Bronitsky 1986). But any tests designed to investigate vessel performance characteristics must be carried out with behaviorally relevant experiments (Schiffer and Skibo 1987; see also Chapter 2). For example, heating effectiveness becomes an important performance characteristic only if at one point in the development of that technology the pottery users were able to discern that a change in properties such as surface treatment or wall composition decreased the time needed for cooking. Moreover, it is not always important that vessels have the best heating effectiveness possible and in some forms of cooking poor heating effectiveness may be desired. Clearly, all tests that investigate performance characteristics must be carried out with some knowledge of subsistence and cooking practices. However, as correlations of finer resolution are made between technological properties and vessel use, a limitation of the approach is highlighted; the intended function of the vessel is too general. What is required are strategies to infer how the vessel was *actually* used.

Actual Vessel Technofunction

Methods that can reconstruct how pots were used in the past have several advantages (see also Rice 1990). First, a study of intended function can provide only a general framework of vessel use (Cackette *et al.* 1987:121; Deal n.d.; Deal and Silk 1988; Schiffer 1989). Although Smith (1988:913-914) defines 14 categories of vessel use, only 4 general types could be employed in his study to correlate vessel shape and size to technofunction. For example, one category referred to as "utility" combines a number of uses that include dry storage, cooking of food (frying or boiling), mechanical processing, serving food, and serving and pouring liquids. This level of generality can be used to address some research questions (e.g., Smith 1988), but for many others it is necessary to have more specific information about vessel use. The second advantage of focusing on actual use of vessels is that many vessels are multifunctional. A Kalinga vegetable and meat cooking pot (*oppaya*) is used for boiling anything that is not rice *and* also for carrying water from the spring to the house. The vessel is probably not constructed with the latter use in mind but it is, nonetheless, an important pottery use activity.

Third, intended use does not always equal actual use. Among the Kalinga, if a rice cooking pot of appropriate size is not available, a vegetable and meat cooking pot could be substituted. In addition, one household in Guina-ang broke their water jar (*immosso*), but they replaced it with a large rice cooking pot. These types of impromptu uses cannot be predicted, or detected, in an analysis of intended technofunction.

Fourth, there is now considerable ethnoarchaeological evidence that pots, no longer being used for their primary function, are frequently employed in a variety of secondary uses (for a review, see Schiffer 1987:25-46). In fact, Deal (1985) documents how contemporary Mayan households curated damaged or fragmented vessels (provisional discard) for secondary use. Only research that reconstructs actual technofunction can determine secondary or tertiary pottery use. Linking alterations of pottery vessels to use activities is the primary means to reconstruct actual technofunction (Rice 1990:5).

Pottery Use Alteration and Technofunction

Matson (1965:204-208), in a discussion of factors that can influence the design of pots used for transporting and storing water, recommends that analysts should not ignore vessel wear patterns, surface treatment, and degree of firing. He suggests that abrasion and scratches on various areas of the vessel provide evidence for use. In addition, Matson mentions that "sludge deposits" in the bottom of water pots should be inspected. Both deletions to a ceramic surface and deposits within the pot, mentioned by Matson, serve as the basis for many of the current pottery use-alteration studies. I will now discuss some of the research that has employed attrition and/or accretion to the ceramic surface to make inferences about vessel use.

There are two general forms of ceramic surface accretion: carbon deposits that result from cooking over an open fire, and residues left by a vessel's contents. The presence of sooting is often used only to discriminate cooking from noncooking vessels (e.g., Blinman 1988:125-129; Hill 1970:49; Nelson and LeBlanc 1986:82; Turner and Lofgren 1966:123). However, in the ceramic analysis performed by Nelson and LeBlanc (1986:123-124), sooting patterns provided additional evidence of pottery use. Relying primarily on surface finish, neck constriction, and sooting patterns, they concluded that the Salado of the Mimbres Valley did not use water vessels. Moreover, the presence of soot on one form of bowl suggested that it was used over a fire, presumably for roasting. Although the work by Nelson and LeBlanc (1986) incorporates a good deal of use-alteration data, only the research by Hally (1983a) and Henrickson (1990; see also Blinman 1988) focuses specifically on use alteration to make inferences about vessel technofunction.

Using ceramic data from two sites in northwestern Georgia, Hally (1983a) identified three forms of use alteration: sooting, oxidation discoloration, and pitting. He found that the soot and oxidation pattern reflected how vessels were positioned in relation to the fire. Abrasion in the form of pitting, which he attributed to some form of physical contact such as stirring or scraping, was also identified in a small number of vessels. Hally then correlated vessel morphology with use traces and was able to make a number of inferences about how vessels were used during the Barnett phase of the Lamar culture.

Henrickson (1990) employed use-alteration data and also morphological and physical properties to infer the original use of a vessel type found at the Chalcolithic site of Seh Gabi in modern Iran. By recording the pattern of both surface abrasions and exterior and interior carbon patterns, Henrickson was able to determine the function of the enigmatic "perforated pots." She concludes that the vessels were used to dry grain or legumes in preparation for storage.

Residues left behind by the contents of vessels is the second general type of accretion. A variety of techniques for identifying residues are now available (see Biers and McGovern 1990; Rice 1987:232-233). For example, animal fats and vegetable oils have been identified through gas chromatography (e.g., Condamin *et al.* 1976; Deal and Silk 1988; Morgan *et al.* 1984; Patrick *et al.* 1985; Rottlander 1990); vessel interiors have been subject to phosphate analysis to determine if the pot held organic material (e.g., Cackette *et al.* 1987; Duma 1972); and an isotopic method (based on ratios of carbon and nitrogen) has been applied to determine the contents of vessels (e.g., DeNiro 1987; Hastorf and DeNiro 1985). Although these strategies show promise, there is still a number of unanswered questions. In particular, it is difficult to discriminate between what was cooked or stored in a vessel from residues that were deposited after the pot was discarded or may have been added as a surface treatment (Rice 1987:233). Moreover, there have been few attempts to evaluate if the identified substances are representative of the items stored or cooked in the pots (Schiffer 1989).

Deposits on vessels, in the form of sooting or residues of the vessel's contents, are important use-alteration traces, but they are somewhat limiting. Sooting can show that cooking took place and the position of the pot on the fire, and interior residues can inform on what was cooked or stored in the vessels. But many vessel technofunctions and certainly many pottery use activities may not form accretions (Schiffer 1989). Vessel surface attrition, however, is a use-alteration trace that has the potential of providing evidence for any type of pottery use activity.

Despite the acknowledgment of the importance of abrasion for determining ceramic use (e.g., Chernela 1969; Matson 1965:204-208), few studies have employed ceramic attritional data, often referred to as "use-wear," in their ceramic analyses. This is unfortunate because ceramic attrition should be able to provide much information about pottery use (Chernela 1969). To date, ceramic abrasion has been used most often to test the proposition that a highly decorated ceramic type such as Mimbres Black-on-white (Bray 1982; Fenner 1977) or White Mountain Redware (Jones 1989) has only nonutilitarian functions. Bray (1982) carried out the most comprehensive study of this kind in her analysis of 124 Mimbres Black-on-white bowls. She found that the vessels served nonutilitarian functions (see also Fenner 1977) and that there is a correlation between degree of precision in design execution and degree of abrasion.

Several other studies (e.g., DeGarmo 1975; Griffiths 1978; Hally 1983a, b; Jones 1989; Kobayashi n.d.) have employed ceramic abrasion to formulate inferences about pottery use. Although DeGarmo (1975:170-173) was unsuccessful in finding links between abrasion and size and decorative classes of pottery, his study is important because it is the first to combine information on vessel shape, technology, and use alteration. Hally's analysis of the Barnett phase ceramics (1983a, 1986) shows how one can employ many sources of information, including morphology, performance characteristics, ethnographic information, context of recovery, and use alteration, to make inferences about pottery use.

The analyses described, though informative, do not yet exploit fully ceramic attrition data. The previous studies focused primarily on the presence or absence of abrasion to infer whether pots were used in activities that required stirring and scraping. However, much more use information can be obtained from pottery attrition.

For example, Griffiths (1978) analyzed eighteenth-century lead-glazed earthenware and was able to discriminate use marks made by knife cuts, fork or spoon scratches, stirring scratches, and beating marks. Moreover, research by Jones (1989; see also Kobayashi n.d.) on the Grasshopper Pueblo pottery collection demonstrates that ceramic attrition is patterned. Abrasion and pitting occurred in various locations on different decorative types and vessel size classes. Drawing inspiration from the same Grasshopper pot collection, Schiffer (1989) proposes a research design in which he calls for the development of a descriptive system of ceramic surface alteration. He provides the framework for a comprehensive surface alteration study on Grasshopper pottery. This would include an analysis of how low-fired ceramics composed of a heterogeneous body, typical of most prehistoric pottery, would abrade under various conditions of wear. The study by Schiffer and Skibo (1989) addressed some of these issues. They set forth a provisional theory of ceramic abrasion in which the basic elements that relate to the rate and nature of abrasion are identified. Basic factors related to abrasion, such as the nature of the ceramic, abrader, and contact situations, are discussed.

Despite the advances made in studying both accretional and attritional ceramic alteration, knowledge about the activities that create use alteration is still incomplete. Moreover, there has not been an integrated study of all forms of use alteration, and there has not yet been a systematic attempt to develop methods to discriminate use alteration from nonuse alteration. The objective of this study is to address these issues. The discussion that follows introduces a framework for doing use-alteration studies that incorporates all forms of ceramic alteration (use and nonuse).

CERAMIC ALTERATION: A FRAMEWORK

This section draws upon the lithic use-wear literature that has burgeoned since Semenov (1964) introduced microwear studies to the West. Because the principles and techniques of lithic use-wear have evolved, a study of pottery use alteration can profit from the years of accumulated knowledge (see also Schiffer 1989). Keeley (1974:322, emphasis his) suggests that a microwear study must "attempt to obtain *precise* designations of functions of the implements examined" and then to "obtain as complete a picture as possible of the total uses represented on implements." However, Keeley (1974:327) recognized, as did Semenov (1964), that many processes, both prior to use (as in manufacture) and in the depositional environment, leave traces that can be confused with those of use. Because this is also true for ceramics, I propose that the term *ceramic alteration* be used as a general category that includes all forms of ceramic use and nonuse alteration.

Ceramic Alteration

Ceramic alteration includes all changes in the ceramic (surface or subsurface) resulting from physical or chemical processes that cause either the addition, deletion, or modification of material (see Table 3.1). Ceramic

Table 3.1. Ceramic Alteration Framework

	Examples	
	Use alteration	*Nonuse alteration*
Carbon deposits	Charring of food, sooting from a fire	Charring or sooting from an unintentional fire
Organic residue	Contents of vessels	Organic matter from the soil
Attrition	Mechanical action of pottery use, non-mechanical action such as salt erosion or thermal spalling	Fluvial abrasion, freeze/thaw breakdown

alteration can occur any time from vessel manufacture to recovery by the archaeologist (extending to processes of analysis and museum curation) and may be created by either use or nonuse processes, or by human or nonhuman agents (cf. Sullivan 1978). For lithic analysts, the nonuse traces are often a source of annoyance, and much research is directed toward distinguishing them from traces of use (see Sala 1986). But because alterations of a ceramic are not confined to the "working edge," as is often the case in lithic use-wear, nonuse alterations do not necessarily hide or confuse traces of use. Moreover, nonuse alterations provide interesting data about the life history of a deposit or a particular vessel. For example, abrasion on sherds can furnish the archaeologist with information regarding the depositional environment such as fluvial transport or trampling (e.g., Buko 1990; Gifford-Gonzalez et al. 1985; McPherron 1967; Skibo 1987).

An unfortunate tendency in experimental lithic use-wear studies is that they are often confined to one particular type of material from an isolated region (Vaughan 1985:9-10). An individual interested in performing a use-wear analysis usually must conduct a series of experiments on replicated tools using local materials relevant to an archaeological case. These studies are often successful but have limited applicability outside that study area—which may be quite restricted geographically. Vaughan (1985) attempted to rectify this situation with a more comprehensive experimental study that would apply to most flint assemblages. It would be unfortunate if pottery use-alteration studies followed the same pattern as the early lithic use-wear research, thereby requiring new experiments for each ceramic assemblage. Certainly, no study can exhaust all surface alteration possibilities, but it is the objective of this research, like that of Vaughan (1985), to provide a more comprehensive treatment of ceramic alteration that focuses on the general principles and processes involved in the production of use and nonuse traces.

A long-standing debate among lithic use-wear analysts is between those who advocate looking at edge polish with high-power microscopy (e.g., Keeley 1980; Semenov 1964) and the analysts who believe the best source of use information is obtained by observing microchipping with low-power magnification (e.g., Odell and Odell-Vereecken 1980; Tringham et al. 1974). To investigate the general processes of use-wear, Vaughan (1985) advocates using a combination of "high-power" and "low-power" techniques. One objective of the present study is to provide the analytical techniques that would enable a ceramic analyst to employ use-alteration data when making inferences about vessel technofunction (actual use). Because this study seeks to understand the general processes involved in ceramic trace formation, I will employ, like Vaughan (1985), a variety of analytical techniques that may be beyond those necessary to make simple correlations between use alteration and the activity that produced it. These techniques are introduced in Chapters 5, 6, and 7.

Nonuse Alteration

A variety of processes from trampling and plowing to freeze-thaw cycles and rodent burrowing can cause nonuse ceramic alteration (for a review of the processes, see Schiffer [1987]). Use alteration requires that a vessel or fragment of a vessel participate in an activity, whereas nonuse alteration implies that a trace is formed while the ceramic is not involved in a purposeful human activity. The life cycle of one cooking vessel can illustrate this point. The pot is first used for cooking, its primary technofunction, where it accumulates a number of use traces. The vessel may crack and begin to leak and then be used to roast beans or coffee (secondary use). If the vessel finally breaks into two pieces, one half may be fashioned into a pot cover, and the other may be used as a scoop (recycling). Eventually, the pot fragments may be thrown away, where they could be scavenged for use in pot firing, picked up by children for use in their courtyard game, or trampled by people and animals. The fragments could then be subject to a number of environmental processes such as fluvial abrasion and freeze-thaw damage. All of these activities that involve people, except trampling, are use alteration. Trampling by people or animals can create distinctive traces, but they are in the category of nonuse alteration. Likewise, a nick on a pot caused by a spoon thrown at a foraging dog (not an uncommon occurrence in Kalinga) is nonuse alteration. Pottery use-alteration activities require that there be an intentional interaction between an individual and a pot or pot fragment. Nonuse ceramic alteration, therefore, includes all environmental formation processes (Schiffer 1987) in addition to a number of cultural processes that involve unintentional interaction between humans and their pots.

Although nonuse ceramic alteration can certainly act as an impediment to investigating use alteration, it can also provide clues about the depositional history of cultural material. For example, evidence for stages of fluvial abrasion on sherds helped to explain the enigmatic distribution of surface sherds in the foothills of the Tortolita Mountains (Skibo 1987). The effects of trampling on the distribution of artifacts has also received some attention (e.g., Gifford-Gonzalez et al. 1985; Nielsen 1991). Moreover, ceramics once in the depositional environment can be altered by a number of physical and chemical processes (Schiffer 1987:143-198). Salt can erode surface treatments (O'Brien 1990), freeze-thaw cycles will exfoliate low-fired sherds, possibly to the point of complete breakdown (Skibo et al. 1989a), moisture can weaken sherds making them more susceptible to erosional processes (Skibo and Schiffer 1987), and chemical changes (additions and deletions) can occur while ceramics are in the depositional environment (Rye 1981:119-120; Schiffer 1987:159-160).

Research has revealed that nonuse ceramic alteration produces a number of distinctive traces that should permit an analyst to identify the process responsible for a given alteration. Important information can be obtained from nonuse ceramic alteration, but because such research is just beginning, the results must be interpreted with caution. The most significant problem is distinguishing use from nonuse alteration. Although the research presented here should be of some help, to avoid confusion, use-alteration studies should, at present, focus on whole or nearly complete vessels. Certainly, this puts a constraint on the assemblages that would be appropriate for use-alteration analysis; many sites—especially in the northern latitudes of North America—do not have a whole vessel assemblage. However, unlike many new analytical techniques, use-alteration studies do not require that improved excavation strategies be devised; the thousands of whole pots in museum storage rooms should provide an endless supply of data for use-alteration studies.

Use Alteration

The term *use alteration* is taken from Hally (1983a). This term is preferred over *use-wear* because as Hally (1983a) demonstrates, a pottery use-alteration study is concerned with both additions and deletions. Although in lithic studies both accretions and deletions are investigated, the term *use-wear* implies an attritional process and is regarded in the present framework as just one form of use alteration. Pottery use alteration is defined as the chemical or physical changes that occur to the surface or subsurface of ceramics as a result of use. These can occur from the moment the vessel emerges from firing to the moment that the use traces are recorded. A potter stacking pots for transport to the market can cause some alteration to the ceramic, as can the handling and storage of a vessel in the museum. Certainly, the objective of most pottery use-alteration studies would be to determine the primary use of the vessel (cooking, storage, etc.), but the broadest framework must be utilized if we are to achieve a complete understanding of pottery use alteration. Moreover, ceramic use-alteration traces can be formed in a variety of pottery use situations. To better understand the interaction of pottery use and use-alteration traces, one must explore further the behavior of ceramic use.

Ceramic Use Behavior

Ceramic use is defined as the intentional interaction of a human and ceramic (vessel or vessel fragment). As mentioned, carrying a pot or using a pot fragment as a tool is ceramic use, but trampling of sherds on the ground (if unintentional) is not. An alteration in the physical or chemical properties of a ceramic (from either use or nonuse processes) is a trace (Sullivan 1978:194). In the following discussion, I am concerned only with pottery vessel use and not the wider issue of ceramic use (which can include use alteration of ceramics that were not once part of vessels such as floor or roof tiles). The formation of traces as a result of pottery vessel use is dependent upon both the nature of the pottery vessel and components of the activity. Pottery use activities are defined in terms of the interaction between the pot and five components of pottery use behavior: contents of the vessel, context of use, time and frequency of use, mode of action, and characteristics of the human participants (cf. Schiffer 1975). Each of these components and the nature of the pottery vessel are now discussed briefly; concrete examples are provided in Chapters 5, 6, and 7.

Use-alteration traces are affected greatly by the nature of the pottery vessel. The nature of the pottery vessel can be described in terms of properties that can include shape, size, weight, hardness, permeability, porosity, surface treatment, and strength. Pottery vessels, as recipients of use-alteration traces, can vary in these and other such properties.

The first general property of a pottery vessel is the characteristic of the fired paste (see also Schiffer and Skibo 1989:105-108). This includes the strength of the fired paste, defined as the resistance to fracture. Though many factors can influence strength, clay composition and firing temperature have the greatest influence. Strength can also change during vessel use, from things such as thermal stress, or while buried in the ground (e.g., freeze-thaw processes). Other characteristics of the fired paste include surface topography, surface treatments, and properties of the temper particles (i.e., hardness, shape, size, quantity, distribution, and orientation). These ceramic properties have the greatest influence on attrition.

Permeability is one ceramic property that I will highlight because it can affect attrition but also the other two forms of use-alteration traces: carbon deposits and organic residues. Permeability can be controlled principally by firing temperature, paste composition, and surface treatment. Research of organic residues, such as the one performed in Chapter 5, requires that the interior pottery surface be permeable; contents of the pot must be absorbed into the vessel wall. Moreover, as described in Chapter 7, both interior and exterior carbon deposition are affected by water that permeates the pottery wall.

The final characteristic of the pottery vessel to be discussed here is shape. The shape of the ceramic surface will influence its susceptibility to attrition and also affect the deposition of carbon. One must be aware of how these properties and all characteristics of the pottery vessel affect trace formation.

The second part in the formation of a pottery use-alteration trace is the activity. Pottery use activities include things such as cooking, roasting, storage, and cleaning. Each of these pottery use activities has five components (see Table 3.2). First, is the characteristics of the user; basically who is doing the activity and all the individual traits of that person. Any pottery use activity, by definition, must involve a human, and this component includes things like the age, sex, or experience of the person and also whether the same person or a variety of people will perform the same activity.

Table 3.2. Use-Alteration Traces and Components of Pottery Use Activity[a]

Components of use activity	Use-alteration traces		
	Organic residue	Carbon deposits	Attrition
User characteristics	−	−	+
Context	−	+	+
Actions	−	+	+
Time/frequency	+	+	+
Contents	+	+	+

[a]The pluses and minuses illustrate whether a use-alteration trace can potentially inform on that component of use activity.

The second component of any pottery use activity is mode of action. This component refers to how the other material objects and the human participant interact with the pottery vessel. Pots are containers used to store liquids, boil, roast, or store various foods. Each type of use entails different modes of action. For example, a pot can be suspended over a fire, placed on the ground in the fire, and variously manipulated while in use. The human participant, the pot, and other objects interact differently with different forms of use.

The third component is the contents of the vessel. Pots are designed to hold material for preparation, storage, transport, or serving. Different pottery use activities are associated with various vessel contents, but most importantly different organic materials will leave characteristic organic traces.

Fourth, the time and frequency of pottery use events are important components of any use activity. The general importance of this variable is that a pot must be used enough times and in long enough durations to create traces. Some traces, like organic residues, will be present after only one use, whereas others, such as attrition, may require multiple uses before use-alteration traces become mapped on to the pottery surface. Moreover, some use-alteration traces, like carbon deposition, will proceed through stages based upon the number of times the pot has been used.

The fifth and final component of any pottery use activity is the context of use. This includes where the activity takes place and any other material object involved in the activity. For example, pots used in the household for family cooking could involve very different activities than vessels used in the courtyard for villagewide cooking. Different people could be involved, different foods could be cooked, and the time and frequency of the use activity may differ significantly. All of these will have an effect on use-alteration traces.

In an archaeological study of pottery use alteration, the objective would be to infer use activity from the three types of traces (carbon deposits, attrition, and organic residues). The important point is that not all use traces can inform on all components of a use activity. Table 3.2 illustrates which of the five components of a use activity can be inferred from carbon deposits, attrition, and organic residues. Note that attrition is the only trace that can potentially inform on all five components of pottery use activity.

One advantage of a pottery use-alteration study is that one can still observe, in an ethnoarchaeological setting, use behavior. Each component of a pottery use activity can be observed and then linked to specific traces. Similar studies with lithic stone tools are not possible, and researchers must rely heavily on experimentation. In this study, experiments and ethnoarchaeological observations are combined. The Kalinga research introduced later describes the ethnoarchaeological data collection strategy.

Chapter *4*

The Pottery
Use-Alteration Study

Beginning in 1973, the Kalinga became the focus of a long-term ethnoarchaeological study (Longacre 1974). Longacre made a year-long study in 1975-1976 and again during 1987-1988 with a field team from the University of Arizona and the University of the Philippines. (For a discussion of Kalinga ethnoarchaeological research, see Graves 1981, 1985, 1991; Longacre 1974, 1981, 1985, 1991b; Longacre and Skibo n.d.; Longacre *et al.* 1991; Stark 1991.)

Longacre's interest in an ethnographic pottery-producing village evolved from his concern with the relationship between social groups and pottery designs. The first case studies of the "new archaeology" (e.g., Deetz 1965; Hill 1970; Longacre 1970) were based on the assumption that as mothers teach daughters pottery making, methods of painting discrete design elements should have intergenerational continuity. Graves (1981, 1985) has demonstrated, using the Kalinga data, that the factors affecting vessel design variation are much more complex than originally envisioned (see also Longacre 1981:60-63). Although Graves (1981, 1985) identified a number of factors that can affect vessel design, the birth cohort of the potter had the strongest influence.

During Longacre's 12-month stay in 1975-1976, a household pottery inventory was made in the villages of Dangtalan and Dalupa. In 1979-1980 Dangtalan was reinventoried, and in 1981 all the houses in Dalupa were visited and the pottery again recorded. In addition to furnishing information about the social context of pottery making, this long-term research provided accurate use-life figures and information about the factors that affect pottery production (Longacre 1985). Long-acre (1985) has compared use-life estimates made by the residents to actual pottery use-life figures and found that informants typically underestimate use life (see also Neupert and Longacre n.d.). The Kalinga morphological data have also been used comparatively to investigate pottery specialization and standardization (Longacre *et al.* 1988). Among the findings was that the potters of Paradijon, a Philippine neighborhood of full-time potters, made more standardized vessel shapes than the part-time household potters from Dangtalan (see also London 1985:189-215).

The most recent field season (1987-1988) focused on some familiar and some new research topics, including pottery production and exchange, pottery use life, economics and its relation to material culture, organization of labor, and the topic of the present study—pottery use alteration. In this chapter, I describe the Kalinga and introduce the village of Guina-ang, home of the use-alteration study. The field data collection strategy is discussed, and pottery use in the village of Guina-ang is described.

THE KALINGA

The Kalinga live within the Cordillera Central, a rugged mountain range in the north-central portion of the Philippine island of Luzon. Although the mountainous terrain has kept them relatively isolated, the Kalinga had significant Western contact beginning with the Spanish shortly after 1600 (Keesing 1962:224-233). This was followed by American, Japanese, and Philippine governmental and/or missionary contact (Keesing and Keesing 1934; for a review, see Graves 1981:100-116). Philippine coastal groups were involved, prior to Western contact, in trade with the Chinese, and porcelain from the Chinese Ming Dynasty (1368-1644) displayed in many Kalinga households demonstrates that they, too, were involved in this exchange, albeit peripherally.

The Kalinga have been the focus of a fair number of ethnographic studies (e.g., Barton 1949; De Raedt 1989; Dozier 1966; Lawless 1977; Takaki 1977; for a review, see Graves 1981). They are described as a separate ethnolinguistic group, among several that occupy northern Luzon, that are organized into endogamous regions. Relations between these regions, composed of tightly clustered villages located among their rice fields along the major rivers, are governed by a series of peace pacts (Bacdayan 1967).

The Kalinga have bilateral descent and neolocal residence although there is a tendency toward matrilocality (Dozier 1966). Villages are usually divided into about three wardlike divisions. Although the divisions are readily recognized by the villagers, the wards possess no political or territorial rights. Currently the primary function of the wards is to help organize villagewide work or ceremonial activities and provide village defense; the young unmarried men of each ward usually sleep in a single house prepared to respond to a village raid (Longacre 1981:52).

The Kalinga household is the basic economic and social unit (Takaki 1977:56; Trostel n.d.). It consists typically of a married couple and their preadult children, but other individuals such as aged parents, unmarried adult children, and newly married children and their spouses are often included in the elementary family unit. Household members usually share a single hearth in a one- or two-room structure. Houses are built on poles so that the primary living area is above the ground level. (Two recently constructed houses in the village of Guina-ang occupy both the raised second floor and the ground floor area.)

Economically, the household is an independent unit. Individual members carry out a substantial portion of the labor and produce of that labor belongs collectively to the household. Rice, the Kalinga staple, comes from fields that are inherited by both husband and wife. Besides rice fields, other primary sources of household wealth include animal ownership and in some cases income acquired by jobs available to a limited number of individuals (e.g., teacher, temporary laborer). There are not, however, great wealth differences. Some obvious examples of poorer households exist (e.g., one-room split-bamboo houses), and some individuals have acquired much wealth from outside labor, but Kalinga villages do not have much wealth differentiation.

The Kalinga participate in a three-tier subsistence economy: irrigated rice field agriculture, swidden cultivation, and hunting and gathering. Rice is the staple and is consumed three times a day. Rice fields are individually owned but are communally worked by a system of balanced labor exchange (Lawless 1977). Two crops of rice are grown each year; the first during the dry season (February-April) and the second in the wet season (May-January). Six varieties of rice are typically cultivated plus one type of sticky rice used to make sweet rice cakes (Lawless 1977). The rice is grown in a series of terraced fields irrigated only by spring water. Dozier (1966) made the distinction between the northern and southern Kalinga based on their reliance on dry-and-wet cultivation of rice. The village of Guina-ang, home for the use-alteration study, falls in the northern Kalinga area and, according to Dozier, should rely on dry cultivation of rice. To my knowledge, no rice is currently grown in swiddens. The reason for the discrepancy is unknown but may be the result of the continuing transition, noted by Dozier (1966; see also Lawless 1977), from dry to wet cultivation of rice. It should be noted that although there is ample land for further rice field terraces, there is not enough water available for irrigating new fields. In the vicinity of Guina-ang, a number of new fields have been abandoned for lack of water.

The other major domesticated plants are coffee and sugar cane. Many households own coffee trees, which are found growing in and around the villages. Coffee, sweetened heavily with sugar, is consumed at every meal. Sugar cane fields are owned by only a few villagers, and the cane is used primarily in making the local wine (*basi*).

The majority of households also have a swidden plot. Individual households are responsible for clearing, planting, and harvesting the swidden field that usually is located in the nearby secondary growth forest. The most common crops are beans (several varieties) and peas (several varieties), but taro, camote, eggplant, squash, leafy vegetables, and tobacco are also grown (see also Lawless 1977).

A variety of native plants and animals also form part of the Kalinga diet. Banana, papaya, coconut, mango, and "star apple" trees grow throughout the village and among the rice fields and are harvested as they become ripe. In addition, numerous wild plants are collected and consumed. Wild animals such as deer, lizards, bats, and a variety of birds are killed for food, but they have now become very scarce near the villages. Ants, bees, locusts, and other insects are also collected and consumed when they are in season. Small fish, eaten dried, and some other aquatic resources are also collected from the rice fields.

Domesticated water buffalo (used also in rice field preparation), pigs, dogs, chickens, and ducks are an additional source of protein. However, water buffalo, pigs, and dogs are owned by a minority of households, and so their consumption is confined to ceremonial occasions at which many individuals consume the meat. Chickens or ducks are owned by about half the households in the village of Guina-ang and are the only source of meat or fowl consumed in a nonceremonial context.

A number of outside food products, such as sugar, flour, oil, and a variety of prepared foods, are also available to the Kalinga. Each village usually has one or more "stores" that carry a limited quantity of some of these products along with items such as cigarettes, soda pop, and alcohol. Villagers can also get outside products from "traveling stores," women who frequent the villages selling food and other products, or by going to the nearest city (Tubuc) where many Western products and locally grown produce are available. Kalinga do not buy many outside goods because of limited cash, not for lack of availability.

THE GUINA-ANG POTTERY USE-ALTERATION STUDY

The use-alteration study took place in the village of Guina-ang (pronounced gee-na-ong) (Figure 4.1). Guina-ang, located in the Pasil Valley, Kalinga-Apayao province (Figure 4.2), is one of three villages that comprised the primary research stations for the Kalinga Ethnoarchaeological Project (Longacre and Skibo n.d.). Guina-ang is a pottery-consuming village unlike the pottery-producing villages of Dalupa and Dangtalan.

Figure 4.1. The village of Guina-ang sits atop a ridge overlooking the Pasil River Valley.

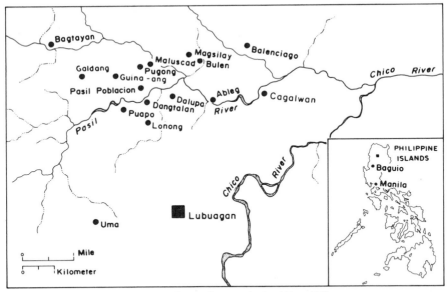

Figure 4.2. Kalinga villages in the Pasil River Valley.

Guina-ang is perhaps the oldest and largest village in the Upper Pasil River Valley; village residents believe that migrants from their village established the communities of Galdang, Pugong, Malacsod, and Dangtalan, known collectively as the "Guina-ang tribe."

Guina-ang, composed of 102 houses, sits atop a ridge that overlooks the Pasil Valley. The villagers recognize four wardlike divisions (see Longacre 1981): Paclang, Dal-log, Siac, and Palittogong (Figure 4.3). Paclang, the northernmost division, is the oldest portion of the barrio, followed by Palittogong, which is located on the southeast end of the village. Dal-log and Siac are the newest portions of the village, built in the memory of the oldest village members. Dal-log and Siac rest on relatively flat ground, but Paclang and Palittogong are on slopes now built into a series of terraces. Some houses are still being built within the main village boundaries, but most of the village expansion is taking place to the south and east of the village. These residents are considered members of Guina-ang, but for the purpose of this research only the houses within the traditional village boundaries, marked by a steep cliff on all sides but near the trail to Galdang, are part of this study.

Guina-ang is often referred to in early Spanish and American ac-

Figure 4.3. Map of the Kalinga village of Guina-ang.

counts (e.g., Carrasco y Perez 1986), although often it is unclear whether the reference is to the village itself or the collection of villages mentioned. The word *Guina-ang* is said to derive from the Kalinga word for trench. Residents recall how a defensive trench was built in the present area of Dal-log to ward off enemies.

Kalinga Pottery

There are three primary types of Kalinga vessels (Figure 4.4): rice cooking (*ittoyom*), vegetable and meat cooking (*oppaya*), and water storage (*immosso*) (for a complete discussion, see Longacre 1981). Rice cooking pots are generally taller, narrower, and have a more restricted aperture than the vegetable/meat cooking pots. The Kalinga recognize three primary sizes of rice cooking pots that can be generally described as small, medium, and large. Vegetable/meat cooking pots, with a larger aperture and more squat appearance than the rice cooking pots, are grouped by the Kalinga into 4 general size classes; the additional class consists of a pot larger than the largest class of rice cooking pots. The water jar (*immosso*) has a restricted neck and comes primarily in one size, although small water jars are made so that young girls can practice carrying pots on their head.

In the Upper Pasil Valley, pots are made in the villages of Dangtalan and Dalupa. Traditionally (as late as the early 1970s), pottery was manufactured primarily for household consumption with only limited exchange. Recently, however, pottery manufacture has shifted, particularly in Dalupa, to production geared more to exchange (Stark n.d.). Pottery manufacture usually takes place during the dry season (February-June), although in Dalupa, a village possibly in the incipient stage of full-time specialization, pottery manufacture continues throughout much of the year. Dangtalan pottery production, in contrast, has been reduced since the early 1970s (Stark n.d.).

Clay is obtained from a number of nearby sources, and in the raw state contains a good deal of nonplastic material. Larger stones may be removed, but no temper is added. The clay is pounded, and water is added until it reaches the proper workability. The pots are made with a

Figure 4.4. Kalinga pottery types. From left to right, water storage jar (*immosso*), rice cooking pot (*ittoyom*), and vegetable/meat cooking pot (*oppaya*).

combination of hand-modeling, coil-and-scrape, and paddle-and-anvil techniques (for a detailed discussion, see Longacre 1981:54-60). First, a wedge of clay is placed on a wooden plate that serves as a rotating platform throughout manufacture. Using a process of scraping and hand modeling, the potter hollows out the wedge and begins to draw up the walls. At this point, clay is scraped from the walls and interior base and formed into short, thick coils. The coils are pinched onto the rising vessel rim as the plate is rotated. When the pot has reached the desired height, the walls are thinned by scraping with fingers or a tool. This process is complete when the surface has become smooth and the vessel walls are the desired thickness. The rim is shaped by grasping the top edge of the pot with a wet rag and rotating the wooden plate with the opposite hand. The rim angle and shape are formed by a technique not unlike that used on a fast wheel. After a short drying period, further shaping may take place, and the potter may stamp and incise the exterior neck as decoration (gili).

When the pot has reached the leather-hard stage, the potter thins the walls further, often by scraping with the sharp edges of a cut metal can. The final stage in the forming process involves shaping the base of the pot with a paddle and anvil. After additional drying, a thin wash of clay is applied to the interior, and additional scraping and smoothing levels out the uneven areas. The pot is then polished with a polishing stone after another short period of drying. This results in pottery surfaces (interior and exterior) that are not lustrous but are very smooth to the touch. A red hematite paint may then be applied with a rag; in Dangtalan rims of the cooking pots near the gili are often painted, but in Dalupa the cooking pots are usually unpainted. Moreover, water jars are typically painted completely red by the Dangtalan potters whereas the Dalupa-made water jars may have a thick hatching on the body or some other stylized design.

When the pots have dried sufficiently, several potters do their firing in a designated place just outside the village. Pots are stacked, mouths faced out, several tiers high with the largest pots at the bottom. Split bamboo, grass, and rice stalks are placed in and around the pots and ignited. The fire is intense but does not last long; the maximum temperature of firings in Dalupa rarely exceeded 700° C (Aronson et al. n.d.), and each firing lasted only about 20 minutes from ignition to pot removal. Immediately after ignition, the potters began poking the fire with bamboo rods to aerate and intensify the fire and to check the color of their firing pots. Pots are removed from the fire while they are still very hot, and a resin (*libo*), obtained from pine trees in the nearby mountains, is applied. The resin comes from a tree, referred to as *lita-o* by the Kalinga, from the family *Pinaceae,* genus *Agathis Philippinensis* (Longacre 1981:60). The interior and exterior of all water jars are coated with the resin (although some Dalupa potters only coat the interior); cooking pots are coated with resin on the interior surface and exterior lip and neck but not on the exterior body.

Field Data Collection Strategy

The use-alteration study was codirected by Masashi Kobayashi and me. Data collection occurred in two phases. The first phase involved a household pottery inventory, pottery use-alteration questionnaire, economic survey, and census. English-speaking Kalinga assistants were trained to collect most of this information. The inventories of household pottery in Guina-ang, Dangtalan, and Dalupa were obtained in a similar manner. Information for each pot, including size, type, when and where obtained, was collected on this form (when the data were collected there were 2,481 ceramic and metal vessels in Guina-ang). A use-alteration form (an example of the household inventory and use-alteration questionnaire is provided in Appendix A) was also filled out in each Guina-ang household. This included information such as which pots were used in the last three meals, who washes the pots, the type of utensils used, when the pot was last used, what the pot is used for, and some use-alteration information.

A second group of Kalinga assistants collected household economic and census information. The economic survey is an abbreviated version of the survey done in Dangtalan (see Trostel n.d.) and includes such information as worth of houses, rice fields, coffee trees, and other possessions. The census form includes the number and ages of all household residents.

Making an accurate map of the village was the final portion of phase one of the data collection. A resident of Dangtalan skilled in cartography (Arnel Delfin) made scale maps of Guina-ang and the other villages in the study.

The second phase of data collection involved observation of pottery use throughout the daily cycle. This involved observing pottery use (e.g., cooking, roasting, water storage, carrying, and cleaning) from before the morning meal (5:30-6:00 A.M.) to the final storage of the pots after the evening meal (6:00-9:00 P.M.). Detailed notes and photographs documented all pottery use activity. Forty households were observed in this manner over a period of about 2 months.

The age of a pot and the frequency of use are also important variables in a use-alteration study. To obtain some data on how the frequency of use affects use alteration, one household agreed to exchange their old vessels for a new set and use the latter exclusively during my stay. Weekly observations were made in this house, and the household members recorded each time a pot was used. Near the end of the research, the "experimental" pots were exchanged for new pots.

Including the full set of pots collected from the experimental household, 189 used pots were collected. New pots purchased in Dangtalan were exchanged for the used vessels. The bulk of the pots was collected from the 40 households in which the more intensive vessel observation occurred. To reduce surface alteration after collection, the pots were immediately wrapped in a Gortex material with a static-free and abrasion-resistant surface. The material also kept the pots dry by allowing gases but not moisture to permeate. To prevent movement of the Gortex wrapping, each vessel was placed into a tight-fitting nylon netting (L'eggs control-top pantyhose size B). The pots were then wrapped in banana bark and rattan, the Kalinga method of pot transport, and carried (on women's heads) to the village of Ableg and the nearest road. A Philippine National Museum truck and crew picked up the pots and made the long journey to Manila. After our Kalinga assistants removed the pots from the banana bark, they were packed into two wooden crates for their journey, by ship, to Los Angeles. A final portion of the journey to Tucson was made by truck. The pots have been catalogued, and they now are curated in the Arizona State Museum. The pots are still wrapped in the Gortex, but the nylon has been removed. Every effort was made to handle the pots as little as possible but, as one can see by this description, some handling was unavoidable. Indeed, there is some evidence of material loss on many of the vessels; but because evidence for material loss is found on the inside surface of the Gortex, an assessment of the alteration can be made and distinguished from use alteration.

Kalinga Pottery Use

Pottery use in the village of Guina-ang occurs in two situations: everyday use and ceremonial use. One group of pots, usually about 4 to 10, is used in daily cooking and is stored near the cooking hearth. Daily cooking and the associated pots form the core of this analysis. Weddings, funerals, fiestas, or occasions that involve volunteer labor are times when a number of the nondaily-use pots would be employed. These vessels are typically stored in the rafters or in areas that are not easily accessible or at least not near the cooking hearth (Figure 4.5).

The Kalinga hearth (Figure 4.6) consists of an approximately square, slightly raised platform (usually about 1 meter or less on a side) of packed earth or in some cases cement that is kept in place by boards. The hearth is usually about 5 to 10 centimeters above the floor, and cooking is done by squatting next to the hearth or sitting on a small stool. During cooking, the pots rest on three supports (*chalpong*) made of fired clay or in some cases stone (several metal fire stands were also observed in Guina-ang). The pot supports are approximately 20 cm high, and they hold the pot about 12 to 17 cm above the hearth surface. Firewood is collected around the village or brought from the swidden fields and can consist of any wood that burns. Hardwood such as coffee is preferred, but the most common wood is *lapachik* or *balbalason,* which are soft, rapidly burning woods. Women, usually the mother or an older daughter, will do the majority of the cooking, although men will cook when necessary. In nearly all households there are occasions when the men must cook because the women are busy with the children or working in the fields.

Pots are usually stored face down on split bamboo or solid plank shelves hung on the kitchen wall (Figure 4.7). Sometimes the pots are stacked, but most often they rest alone, face down in a single or double row. Metal pots (*carderos*), now used a great deal in Kalinga kitchens, are usually

Figure 4.5. Nondaily-use cooking vessels stored on rafters near the roof of the house.

Figure 4.6. Kalinga kitchen and hearth.

hung by their handles near the pottery shelf. When pots are in use but not on the fire, they usually rest on pot rings made of rattan (Figure 4.8).

Figure 4.7. Daily-use cooking pots stored on a shelf near the hearth.

Figure 4.8. Pots in use but not on the fire are often placed on rattan rings.

Cool pots are picked up and carried usually by the rim, and hot vessels are carried with a rattan carrier (Figure 4.9) that grasps the pot around

Figure 4.9. Hot cooking pots are taken off the fire with a rattan carrier.

the neck. Hot pots are usually carried only a short distance, either to a rattan pot ring or to the side of the hearth.

Three meals are cooked in a typical day, though the noon meal may be prepared and eaten at the rice fields or swidden plots. A set of pots, usually heavily used or cracked household vessels, is kept at the fieldhouses. Every meal consists of rice and usually some type of vegetable or meat. Meat is consumed infrequently, so the contents of the vegetable/meat pots typically consist of vegetables grown in the gardens or swiddens or collected in the areas surrounding the village. In the majority of households, rice is cooked in metal pots, and the vegetables and meat are cooked in ceramic vessels. Nearly every household has enough metal pots for all their cooking, but they prefer clay pots for cooking vegetables and meat.

Rice is consumed though not necessarily cooked at every meal. Rice remaining from the previous meal is usually heated and eaten; if leftovers are insufficient, more rice is cooked either in an *ittoyom* or a metal pot. First, the proper amount of rice is measured, which depends on the number of people at the meal, and then rinsed in another pot (ceramic or metal). Rice is measured by a standardized unit (*chupa*) that is roughly 350 cc. A pot of appropriate size is then selected, also based on size as measured by *chupas,* and a layer of interwoven leaves (*appin*) is placed inside (Figure 4.10). The leaves keep the rice from sticking, either to the ceramic or metal pot, making washing easier. The rice is transferred to the cooking pot by scooping it out of the rinse pot by hand. Ideally, the boiled rice should completely fill the pot (to the neck of a ceramic pot and to just below the rim in a metal pot).

The rinsed rice is put in the pot, and water is filled to the neck of the *ittoyom* and to just below the rim of a metal pot (Figure 4.11). The pot is covered with a metal cover (metal covers, which are borrowed from the metal pots, have completely replaced the traditional ceramic lids). A large fire is built under the rice pot, and it quickly becomes covered by a dull gray soot (Figure 4.12). The pot is usually left unattended until boiling or just before boiling. As the rice comes to a boil, the cover may be lifted off several times and the rice may be loosened with the handle of a wooden spatula (*edjus*) (Figure 4.13). Soon after the rice boils (usually from about 15 to 25 minutes), the pot is removed (ceramic pots are taken off with the rattan carrier) and put next to the fire on the hearth soil, referred to here as the *simmer position* (Figure 4.14). Before the pot

Figure 4.10. A layer of interwoven leaves is often placed inside rice cooking vessels.

Figure 4.11. Rice cooking pots are filled with water to the neck prior to cooking.

Figure 4.12. A rice pot on the fire soon becomes covered with a dull gray soot.

Figure 4.13. Right before the rice is taken off the fire, it is loosened with a ladle handle.

Figure 4.14. The rice cooking pot (on left) sits next to the fire on a bed of coals, whereas the vegetable/meat pot sits on the fire.

is taken off, coals from the fire are placed in the simmer position. The pot will sit here, within an inch or so of the fire, while the other food is cooked. During this period it is rotated, about a third of a turn, usually three or four times. The pot is taken out of the simmer position and put on a rattan pot ring or directly on the hearth soil but off the coals. It is tilted slightly and rotated while the rice is removed with a wooden spatula (*edjus*) (Figure 4.15).

Vegetable or meat cooking, almost always done in the ceramic pot (*oppaya*), does not follow as consistent a pattern as the rice cooking because of the many types of food that are cooked. For example, some items that take a long time to cook (e.g., beans and peas) are boiled both before and after cooking the rice. But the typical pattern is to cook the vegetables or meat while the rice cooking vessel is in the simmer position. Unlike rice cooking, usually only about one-third to one-half of the vessel is filled with water (Figure 4.16). Moreover, the vegetable/meat pots are typically on the fire longer than rice cooking pots. The objective in vegetable/meat cooking is to bring the contents to a boil and then let the pot simmer at the boiling point until cooking is done. Vegetable/meat

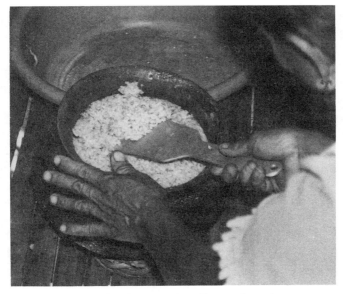

Figure 4.15. Removing rice with a wood spatula.

cooking pots require a bit more attention by the cook than rice pots; the pot may be covered and uncovered many times, and water may be added

Figure 4.16. A vegetable/meat pot sits on the fire half-filled with water.

frequently and the contents stirred. The fire is also more closely monitored; it must be hot enough to keep the pot boiling but not so intense that the pot will boil over. Despite the care taken, boilovers are frequent. When the contents are cooked, the pot is removed with the rattan carrier and usually placed on a rattan pot ring or directly on the hearth soil. The vegetable or meat is then served usually with a ladle made of coconut shell (Figure 4.17).

Another common pottery use activity is roasting. A cooking pot that is no longer thought suitable for its primary function because it is cracked or otherwise worn out may be used to roast coffee (primarily) but also beans, peas, or chilies. Roasting any item involves the same use behavior. The pot is placed on the supports (*chalpong*) at a 45° angle (Figure 4.18). A moderately hot fire is built, and the coffee beans or another item is placed in the pot. While the pot is on the fire, the contents are stirred continuously with a wooden spatula (Figure 4.18). The roasting pot, never washed, is usually stored above the hearth on the firewood drying rack.

The water pot (*immosso*) is the final pot used on a daily basis. Plastic containers have replaced *immosso* in some cases, but the vast majority of

Figure 4.17. Removing the vegetables with a wood ladle.

Figure 4.18. Roasting coffee in a worn-out rice cooking pot.

households still use the ceramic pots, possibly because of their ability to keep the water cooler through evaporative cooling. Water jars usually sit on a rattan ring on a shelf in the kitchen area (Figure 4.19). The pots are almost always covered by an enameled metal plate, and a single enameled dipping cup most often rests on the plate. Water jars are filled by either taking them to the nearby village water source or by bringing water back in cooking pots after cleaning.

Washing is the final pottery use activity to be discussed. After the morning and midday meals, pots along with the other eating utensils are carried to one of five Guina-ang water sources (Figure 4.20). Water is supplied to Guina-ang by pipe from a natural spring located above the village. For the journey, the pots are either stacked in a metal basin with the other items to be washed, or they are carried by the rim, sometimes two in one hand. Both the rice and vegetable/meat cooking pots are washed basically in the same manner (pottery washing is discussed in more detail in Chapter 6). The exteriors are cleaned by placing them on their side directly on the ground; the pot is scrubbed with one hand while rotating it with the other (Figure 4.21). A mixture of sand, *appin* leaves, charcoal, a wet rag, and sometimes soap is held in the hand for

Figure 4.19. A water jar sits on a rattan ring on a kitchen shelf. A dipping cup sits on a metal plate that covers the water jar.

scrubbing. The interior is washed by putting the pot on the ground at a 45° angle and again scrubbing with one hand and rotating with the other (Figure 4.22). Washing is usually concluded with a water rinse; this involves rapidly scrubbing the pot (with no sand, charcoal, etc.) while holding it in the air by the rim and spinning it repeatedly (Figure 4.23). Pots are either carried back to the house in the same wash basin, or they are filled with water to replenish the household's water jar. A filled pot is often carried back on the woman's head; a towel or woven pot rest helps to balance one or possibly two or three stacked pots (Figure 4.24).

This discussion should provide the reader with a general impression of Kalinga pottery use and the data collection strategy. Through this description of Kalinga life and the more detailed information provided in

Figure 4.20. A woman carries out dirty pots and other dishes to the water source for washing.

the subsequent chapters, it should be clear that pottery use is very patterned. Repeated pottery use behavior does leave use-alteration traces on the vessels. The following chapters describe the correlation between pottery use activities of cooking pots and the three forms of use-alteration traces: organic residue, soot, and attrition. Though there are informative use-alteration traces on water jars and roasting pots, this study focuses on the 4 to 10 cooking pots used in households on a daily basis. I choose to focus on daily-use cooking vessels only because, unlike water jars, they possess the three forms of use-alteration traces.

Figure 4.21. Washing the exterior of a cooking pot.

Figure 4.22. Washing the interior of a cooking pot.

Figure 4.23. Rinsing the pot after scrubbing.

Figure 4.24. Carrying pots filled with water back to the house.

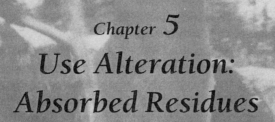

Chapter **5**
Use Alteration:
Absorbed Residues

Sophisticated analytical techniques have had mixed results in archaeology. Some techniques, like carbon-14 dating, have become commonplace—and indispensable—in archaeological analysis, whereas others come and go with little effect. Part of this problem can be attributed to the lack of communication between archaeologists and those in the "hard" sciences; many new techniques are simply not applied to issues that interest archaeologists (see De Atley and Bishop 1991 for a discussion of these issues). But I am certain that most archaeologists would immediately see the usefulness of a technique that could determine what was cooked or stored in a ceramic vessel.

After the introduction of agriculture, pottery and fragments of pots are the most ubiquitous material culture recovered. A method to determine accurately what pottery vessels once contained would be a tool of enormous potential. But for a prehistorian to invest in a potentially expensive technique, two requirements must be met: (1) it must be demonstrated that the technique is accurate, and (2) it must be presented in a way that will make it possible for archaeologists to integrate it easily into their research. The purpose of this chapter is to address these two issues. Using Kalinga data, one technique for analyzing food residues in pottery is explored. Fatty acids are extracted from pots of known use to examine the correlation between what was cooked in the pot and the remaining fatty acids. In addition, sherds from an excavated Kalinga midden were studied to better understand fatty acid preservation.

Organic contents of prehistoric vessels can be identified with various analytical techniques (see Biers and McGovern 1990), but three methods are most common. The first focuses on the phosphorous content of the vessel wall. Duma (1972) introduced this technique in archaeology, and Cackette *et al.* (1987) have recently built upon Duma's work with an analysis of a small ethnographic collection of cooking vessels. The basic premise of this research is that phosphorus, present in all plants and animals, should be absorbed into a vessel wall through a permeable surface. Thus pottery surfaces that have had contact with organic matter should yield higher phosphorus levels. The presence of phosphorus, however, suggests only that pottery once contained organic material; individual plant or animal species cannot be identified. In addition, the research requires that one determine—and then compensate for—the phosphorus levels that occur in the potting clay and the sediments that surrounded the vessel in the depositional environment. Dunnell and Hunt (1990) reevaluated this technique and found that these and other issues make it an unpromising method for inferring vessel contents. It is possible that under certain circumstances variation in sherd phosphorus content can lead to inferences about pottery use, but at present there are less problematic techniques that can result in more specific identifications of former pot contents.

The second residue technique, isotope analysis, does have the potential to identify what was cooked in a vessel, and some have found success with this technique (see Deal n.d., 1990; DeNiro 1987; Hastorf and DeNiro 1985; Morton and Schwarcz 1988). This method is based on the fact that plants can be identified by carbon and nitrogen ratios. Although there is still some basic research to be done before isotope analysis becomes a common archaeological tool, the biggest drawback is that the analysis requires carbonized food encrustations on the vessel surface. Unfortunately, such residues are not found on all cooking vessels, and carbonized encrustations are never present on pots that do not typically contact heat or flame, such as storage containers.

The final form of residue analysis, and the focus of this chapter, concentrates on fatty acids. Fatty acids have a number of unique qualities that make them particularly suitable as a means for determining the original contents (use) of pottery vessels. Fatty acids are absorbed in vessel walls, and visible encrustations are not necessary (although they can be analyzed). Moreover, unlike phosphorus levels, combinations of fatty acids can be linked to specific plants and animals. Fatty acids are valuable for residue analysis because (1) they occur in different combinations and in different proportions in every plant and animal species, (2) they survive normal cooking temperatures, and (3) fatty acids can survive (although not without some change) long periods in the depositional environment.

Condamin *et al.* (1976) were the first to introduce fatty acid analysis to the study of archaeological ceramics. Using a combination of gas chromatography and mass spectrometry (GC/MS), they tested for the presence of olive oil in samples from an excavated amphora, a Mediterranean storage jar. The combinations and ratios of fatty acids suggested that the jars were used for storage of olive oil. The Condamin *et al.* (1976) study is important because it demonstrates that fatty acids can penetrate a vessel wall and that fatty acids can survive unchanged over long periods in the depositional environment (see also Nakano 1989a).

The Condamin *et al.* (1976) study was, in several ways, well suited for fatty acid analysis. The material, olive oil, consists almost entirely of fatty acids, and it is a liquid that can easily penetrate a pot's surface. The amphora was probably used only for olive oil storage; it was never subject to the heat of a cooking fire; and the depositional environment appeared to be well suited to fatty acid preservation.

Other investigators such as Deal and Silk (1988), Marchbanks (1989), Hill and Evans (1989), Patrick *et al.* (1985), and Rottlander (1990) have attempted to apply this strategy to the more complex problem of identifying the former contents of cooking vessels. Patrick *et al.* (1985) looked at the residue adhering to fragments of pottery excavated from a shell-midden site on the southwestern Cape of South Africa. They conclusively determined that the fatty acids were of animal rather than plant origin, but attempts to identify the animal species were not completely successful. The ratios of palmitic to stearic acid suggested to them that the fatty acids were of marine origin, possibly seal. Patrick *et al.* (1985) ran several experiments to replicate cooking and postuse fatty acid decomposition. They found that the fatty acids changed slightly, but the ratios between the important fatty acids did not.

Hill and Evans (1987, 1989), in an analysis of Micronesian pottery, advocate using a variety of analytical techniques to look at not only fatty acids but an array of organic constituents. Their research, primarily employing infrared spectroscopy, has identified chemical signatures for many Pacific cultigens. They also have had some success in identifying the cultigens in the residues of prehistoric sherds. Interestingly, Hill and Evans (1989) found little evidence for either the breakdown of the residues or the introduction of contaminants while in the depositional environment; this topic is taken up later.

In perhaps the most involved analysis of fatty acids absorbed in North American pottery, Marchbanks (1989) analyzed 100 sherds from a Caddoan site in central east Texas. In addition to making some correlations between the absorbed fatty acids and some basic food groups, he did a preliminary analysis of how fatty acids decompose in the depositional environment and when exposed to normal cooking temperatures. The importance of Marchbanks's research, however, is his extraction technique and the method of characterizing fatty acids (see later discussion).

Japanese archaeologists have also carried out routinely analyses of fatty acids on pottery and stone tools (e.g., Nakano 1989a, b). Nakano (1989a), a leader in this field, has done extensive research on how fatty acids change as a result of long-term burial and exposure to normal cooking temperatures.

At the University of Tubingen, Germany, Rottlander (1990; Rottlander and Schlichtherle 1978, 1983) and his colleagues have been involved in a long-term study of residual fats in archaeological pottery. Their research focuses on the two critical components of fatty acid research: linking fatty acid profiles to specific plants and animals and the decomposition of fats.

Similarly, Deal and Silk (1988) analyzed archaeological sherds, soils associated with the sherds, replicated ceramic bricks impregnated with beaver, yellow perch and white-tailed deer fat, and a set of control samples to explore the factors that can affect fatty acid absorption and preservation. Deal and Silk (1988) did not find clear links between the archaeological sherds and the fatty acid profiles of the experimental specimens. However, they did find evidence of adipocere, which is the product of fatty acid hydrolysis (fatty acid breakdown is discussed in more detail later). They also note the problems of using fatty acid residue analysis to identify specific plants or animals in pots that were used for cooking multiple items or that were used for other functions (see also Heron *et al.* 1991a). Deal and Silk (1988:116-117) note that these problems need to be resolved before the study of absorbed fats becomes a useful tool in archaeology. They suggest a combined experimental and ethnoarchaeological study to resolve the problems, and many of their suggestions are incorporated into the analysis described later.

The analysis of absorbed residues on the Kalinga pottery focuses on several issues. First, the Kalinga vessel corpus provides the opportunity to investigate, with a large sample, whether absorbed residues accurately reflect what was boiled in the cooking vessels. The greatest success in fatty acid analysis thus far has been obtained with storage vessels (Condamin *et al.* 1976); less clear results have been obtained with cooking pots (e.g., Deal and Silk 1988; Patrick *et al.* 1985). Although some experimental research suggests that fatty acids are likely to survive normal cooking temperatures (cf. Nakano 1989a:116; Rottlander and Schlichtherle 1983), the Kalinga study can examine this notion under real cooking conditions.

Second, this investigation explores how fatty acid profiles appear in vessels that are used to cook a number of plants and animals. It is important to know if the fatty acids represent the item last cooked or are an amalgam of the various vegetables and meats cooked during the vessel's use life. If the fatty acids do implicate a variety of items, it will be important to explore what—if anything—can be said about the specific plants or animals.

Third, the effects of the depositional environment need to be investigated. Fatty acids do survive long periods in the depositional environment but not without some change (Nakano 1989a; Rottlander and Schlichtherle 1983). In the present study, changes in absorbed fatty acids are also considered.

ANALYSIS OF ABSORBED RESIDUES

A several-stage sampling strategy was employed in the Kalinga case study. The first stage involves testing of a control group that consists of an unused pot, the resin applied to the interior surfaces, a rice sample, five types of common Kalinga vegetables, and two types of meat. The second stage includes residue samples removed from six rice-cooking (*ittoyom*) and five vegetable/meat cooking pots (*oppaya*). Prior to collection, vessels selected for the analysis were part of a household's daily-use pottery assemblage. No other selection criteria were used except that refitted broken pots were chosen when possible (a small number of pots were broken in transit).

The Kalinga cooking vessels provide an interesting contrast because the rice cooking pots are used only to cook rice (with few exceptions), whereas vegetable/meat cooking pots boil all other foods. This first portion of the sampling investigates simple correlations between what was cooked and the absorbed residues.

The third and final stage of the residue analysis is done with Kalinga "archaeological sherds" to explore the preservation of fatty acids when sherds are in a depositional environment. A midden was excavated during the 1976 field season in the Dangtalan "sitio" of Puapo. Ten recovered sherds are tested to see how well the fatty acid profiles match those of the currently used pottery collection. The age of the sherds is unknown, but designs on many of them are not made by current potters.

Fatty Acid Chemistry

Before proceeding further, it is necessary to briefly introduce the chemistry of fatty acids and some of the nomenclature used (see Aurand *et al.* 1987; Braverman 1963; Christie 1989; Gunstone and Norris 1983; Hitchcock and Nichols 1971). Edible fats along with carbohydrates and proteins are the most important food nutrients. Fats belong to a class of substances known as "lipids," which are insoluble in water and are derived from aliphatic carboxylic acids—commonly known as fatty acids. There are three main groups of lipids: (1) fats and oils, consisting of triglycerides, or neutral glycerides; (2) waxes, composed of fatty acids esterified by long-chained monohydric alcohols rather than glycerol; and (3) phospholipids that consist of compounds in which glycerol is esterified by fatty acids and phosphoric acids and other compounds. Lipids are most abundant in specific tissues, such as seeds and fruits, but they occur in all parts of plant and animal tissue. Edible fats are mixtures of triglycerides, which are formed by the esterification of glycerol and fatty acids, and small amounts of other matter such as sterols, pigments, and trace metals.

Most naturally occurring fatty acids consist of even numbers of carbon atoms with attached hydrogen atoms (anywhere from 2 to 36 or more). They usually occur in straight chains, with a carboxyl group at one end, and there may be one or more double bonds between carbon atoms. Fatty acids without double bonds are referred to as saturated and those with one or more double bonds are mono- or polyunsaturated, respectively. Three systems of nomenclature are commonly used to refer to fatty acids: the systematic name, trivial name, and a shorthand designation. For example, one of the most common fatty acids has a trivial name of *palmitic* because it is the principal constituent of palm oil. The systematic name is *hexadecanoic,* which reveals to the chemist that it has 16 carbon atoms and no double bonds. The shorthand designation, used in this study, would be 16:0; the first figure refers to the number of carbon atoms and the second the number of double bonds (see Table 5.1 for a list of the systematic, trivial, and shorthand designations of all fatty acids discussed in this chapter). Although there are many fatty acids, the most abundant in plant and animals are those with 14, 16, or 18 carbon atoms. Nearly all living tissue has 16:0 and 18:0, and the most common unsaturated fatty acid is 18:1. The identifying feature of plant and animal species is that these common groups occur in different proportions, and some of the minor fatty acids, such as 18:3, occur in trace amounts and can act as signatures of a particular species.

Sampling Methods

The process of extracting fatty acids from a vessel fragment can be performed with just a few simple instruments. Although others have used more elaborate extraction techniques, after a bit of experimentation it was discovered that a much simpler strategy was effective. The sample from

Table 5.1. Common Fatty Acids

Systematic name	Trivial name	Shorthand designation
Ethanoic	Acetic	2:0
Butanoic	Butyric	4:0
Hexanoic	Caproic	6:0
Octanoic	Caprylic	8:0
Decanoic	Capric	10:0
Dodecanoic	Lauric	12:0
Tetradecanoic	Myristic	14:0
Hexadecanoic	Palmitic	16:0
Octadecanoic	Stearic	18:0
Eicosanoic	Arachidic	20:0
Docosanoic	Behenic	22:0
Tetracosanoic	Lignoceric	24:0
9-Hexadecenoic		16:1
9-Octadecenoic	Oleic	18:1
9,12-Octadecadienoic	Linoleic	18:2
9,12,15-Octadecatrienoic		18:3
11-Eicosenoic		20:1

the whole pots was removed by drilling out a 1-inch-diameter plug with a diamond-edged coring tool. A low-speed electric drill was used, and a stream of distilled water was applied to the coring area with a hand sprayer. The sample was removed from the base of the pot, and all possible hand contact with the interior surface was avoided. The Kalinga archaeological sherds have been stored in plastic bags since 1976. In an attempt to sample cooking vessels, only sherds with exterior sooting were selected for the analysis.

The area to be sampled was first scraped lightly with a stainless steel spatula and rubbed gently with a laboratory wipe ("kim-wipe"). This preliminary step was taken to avoid as many contaminants as possible (i.e., contaminates from the soil, human hands, or anything that came in contact with the pottery surfaces). To collect the sample, the same spatula was used to scrap material from about a 2-cm-diameter area from what had been the interior surface of the vessel. Usually about half of the thickness of the sample was removed or about 1 to 3 mm. The fine powder was then mixed with approximately 30 ml of methanol (Reagent Grade) and placed on a magnetic stirrer/hotplate for a minimum of 5 minutes. The specimen was heated to approximately 50° C, just below the boiling point of methanol, to increase solubility. After removal from the heater/stirrer, the mixture was set aside for several minutes to permit the particulate matter to settle out. Approximately 5 ml aliquots were taken by pipette from the top of the solution, to avoid particulate matter, and placed into glass sample vials.

The control samples of food and resin were simply ground to a powder with a mortar and pestle (except the meat, which was cut into small pieces) and then put through the same process as described. The samples were submitted to the Mass Spectrometry Facility at the University of Arizona. Details of the gas chromatography/mass spectrometry procedures are provided in Appendix B.

Results

The extraction procedure proved to be very successful; fatty acids appeared in all used pottery and archaeological sherds. Characterization of the samples, based on fatty acid profiles, was done by calculating ratios of the most common fatty acids (16:0, 18:0, and 18:1) and also noting the presence of "signature" fatty acids. Marchbanks (1989) argues that a more accurate method of characterizing fatty acids is by relative percentage of saturated fats (%S). The use of this figure (%S) to characterize the fatty acid profile is based on the fact that animals usually have more saturated fats than plants. However, in his study the instability of some saturated fatty acids required that the %S figure be calculated with only 12:0 and 14:0. In the present study, the %S figure cannot be used because too many of the samples did not have 12:0 or 14:0.

Controls

To provide background control for the analysis, an unused pot, resin used to coat the interior of Kalinga vessels, the methanol used to extract the fatty acids, and a reagent blank (the GC/MS run without a sample) were analyzed for fatty acids. The resin and the methanol had no fatty acids. The reagent blank yielded a small amount of 16:0 and some other unidentified fatty acids but not in amounts significant enough to compromise the subsequent analysis. The unused pot, which combines the contaminants seen in the reagent blank and the organics in the clay, had trace amounts of 16:0 and 18:0. All of the pottery samples with fatty acids had amounts of 16:0 and 18:0 that were much greater than the trace amounts in the unused pot. Moreover, these background figures should be relatively constant, assuming the same solvent, GC column and pottery type are used, and should not influence the analysis.

The rice, vegetable, and meat samples all have unique fatty acid profiles (see Table 5.2, and 5.3, and Figure 5.1). Rice is characterized by a low 18:0 to 16:0 ratio (18:0/16:0) and a 18:1/16:0 value that is near 1. These ratios along with the presence of 14:0 distinguish rice. Similar fatty acid profiles for rice can be found in the literature (e.g., Hilditch and Williams 1964; Food Composition Tables for the Near East).

In contrast to rice, four of the five Kalinga vegetables lacked 18:1 or had very low 18:1/16:0 values. In all but Vegetable 4 (see Table 5.3), the 18:0/16:0 values were greater than the 18:1/16:0 values. Vegetable 4 has a profile that is similar to rice except that the value for 18:1/16:0 is lower for the former. Figure 5.1 clearly illustrates that rice and vegetables can be discriminated based upon the ratios of 16:0, 18:0, and 18:1. The common feature of all the vegetables (including rice) is the high percentage of polyunsaturated fats. In all but Vegetable 1, polyunsaturated fats are the first or second most common acid.

Two meats commonly cooked in the *oppaya* are chicken and pork. A sample of U.S. commercial chicken and pork (bacon) were run through

Table 5.2. Fatty Acid Percentages[a]

Fatty acid	Samples					
	Rice	Veg 1	Veg 2	Veg 3	Veg 4	Veg 5
2:0						
6:0						
10:0						
12:0						
14:0	0.88	2.01				
16:0	22.62	6.63	28.44	30.42	29.81	31.72
18:0	5.09	3.04	4.02	9.18	7.70	7.44
20:0	1.57			1.55		1.76
22:0						4.71
24:0						2.14
16:1						
18:1	26.60	1.52			21.03	
18:2	41.54			52.91	27.16	52.20
18:3			64.21			
20:1	0.82					
Other[b]	0.84	86.80	3.30	5.92	14.26	

Fatty acid	Samples				
			Rice cooking pots		
	Chicken	Pork	H92P4	H101P6	H92P13
2:0					
6:0					
10:0				3.10	
12:0			1.30	34.07	20.71
14:0		3.63	2.29	25.37	12.54
16:0	23.89	21.21	19.03	18.34	22.99
18:0	9.17	9.09	4.76	6.84	5.16
20:0			1.31		
22:0					
24:0			1.01		
16:1	8.55	4.48	1.83		
18:1	35.27	44.99	18.49	9.34	16.39
18:2	19.89	16.58			5.01
18:3					
20:1					
Other	3.23		49.98	2.91	17.15

Fatty acid	Samples				
	Rice cooking pots			Vegetable/meat cooking pots	
	H102P19	H92EXP2	H92EXP7	H99P12	H92EXP1
2:0				1.80	
6:0					3.29
10:0					
12:0	18.05	6.33			32.18
14:0	10.62	5.42			27.23

Table 5.2. Fatty Acid Percentages[a] (continued)

| | Samples | | | | |
| | Rice cooking pots | | | Vegetable/meat cooking pots | |
Fatty acid	H102P19	H92EXP2	H92EXP7	H99P12	H92EXP1
16:0	32.87	40.08	14.39	45.21	17.08
18:0	8.21	6.58	3.55	29.11	6.57
20:0					
22:0					
24:0					
16:1		2.26			
18:1	11.78	39.30	8.96	2.64	9.16
18:2					
18:3					
20:1					
Steroid				0.82	
Other	18.44		73.08	20.42	4.46

| | Samples | | | | | |
| | Vegetable/meat cooking pots | | | Excavated sherds | | |
Fatty acid	H92EXP3	H84P12	H84P7	ArchS1	ArchS2	ArchS3
2:0						
6:0						
10:0						
12:0	32.61	4.61			3.37	
14:0	17.31	3.66		4.66	4.31	
16:0	12.94	18.74	35.11	10.52	24.44	7.07
18:0	5.20	24.70	17.24	6.21	13.95	
20:0						
22:0						
24:0						
16:1		3.04				
18:1	3.87	19.51	37.51	3.28	11.13	
18:2		4.64		2.89	2.51	
18:3						
20:1						
Other	28.03	21.04	10.12	72.39	40.22	

| | Samples | | | | | | |
| | Excavated sherds | | | | | | |
Fatty acid	ArchS4	ArchS5	ArchS6	ArchS7	ArchS8	ArchS9	ArchS10
2:0							
6:0							
10:0							
12:0				2.78		1.64	
14:0	3.41	2.51	4.62	4.77	2.87	4.03	5.87
16:0	10.29	3.58	12.92	22.68	10.00	12.78	10.22
18:0	5.00	1.68	5.90	6.63	3.19	4.48	3.85
20:0							

Table 5.2. Fatty Acid Percentages[a] (continued)

Fatty acid	Samples						
	Excavated sherds						
	ArchS4	ArchS5	ArchS6	ArchS7	ArchS8	ArchS9	ArchS10
22:0						2.33	
24:0							
16:1			2.77	3.71		2.78	3.60
18:1		1.38	4.56	10.69	2.85	3.77	3.44
18:2				3.98			
18:3							
20:1							
Other	81.47	90.74	69.16	44.70	81.00	68.09	72.29

[a]Note that these percentages are only relative figures.
[b]Consists primarily of nonfatty acid chemicals; high figures in this category are related to the adjustment of the GC/MS.

the GC/MS to serve as further controls. The pork and chicken can be distinguished from the plants in several ways. Figure 5.1 illustrates that chicken and pork have very different ratios of 16:0, 18:0, and 18:1 than the plants (see also Table 5.3). In addition, a signature fatty acid, 16:1, is also present in both the pork and chicken but not in the plants (Table 5.2). Note also in Table 5.2 that the meats have a much lower percentage of polyunsaturated fats than the plants.

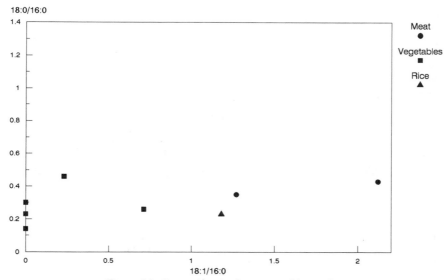

Figure 5.1. Fatty acid ratios (meat, vegetables, rice).

Table 5.3. Ratios of Major Fatty Acids

Source	18:0/16:0	18:1/16:0
Rice	0.23	1.18
Vegetable 1	0.46	0.23
Vegetable 2	0.14	0.00
Vegetable 3	0.30	0.00
Vegetable 4	0.26	0.71
Vegetable 5	0.23	0.00
Pork	0.43	2.12
Chicken	0.35	1.27
H94 P4 (Rice pot)	0.22	0.69
H101 P6 (Rice pot)	0.37	0.51
H92 P13 (Rice pot)	0.22	0.71
H102 P19 (Rice pot)	0.25	0.36
H92 Exp2 (Rice pot)	0.16	0.98
H92 Exp7 (Rice pot)	0.25	0.62
H99 P12 (Vegetable/meat pot)	0.64	0.06
H92 Exp1 (Vegetable/meat pot)	0.38	0.53
H92 Exp3 (Vegetable/meat pot)	0.40	0.30
H42 P7 (Vegetable/meat pot)	0.49	1.07
H84 P12 (Vegetable/meat pot)	1.32	1.04
ArchS 1	0.59	0.31
ArchS 2	0.57	0.46
ArchS 3	0.00	0.00
ArchS 4	0.49	0.00
ArchS 5	0.47	0.00
ArchS 6	0.46	0.35
ArchS 7	0.29	0.47
ArchS 8	0.32	0.29
ArchS 9	0.35	0.29
ArchS 10	0.38	0.34

But chicken and pork also each have unique fatty acid features. The chicken is characterized by a low 18:0/16:0 value and a ratio of 18:1/16:0 that is near 1 (see Table 5.2). The unique feature of pork is that it is dominated by 18:1.

Rice Cooking Pots

The cooking process may destroy some fatty acids. Mono- and polyunsaturated fats, especially 18:2 and 18:3, that are present in the raw foods are not usually detected in the vessel walls after cooking. The disappearance of the mono- and polyunsaturated fats may also be the result of oxidation (discussed later); the residue analysis began about 1 year after the pots were last used. Only 18:1, which is apparently a very stable fatty acid (cf. Rottlander and Schlichtherle 1983), consistently survives the cooking process. The fate of the mono- and polyunsaturated fats is not known, but it appears that they break down into various nonfatty acid (and perhaps fatty acid) constituents.

The fatty acid profiles of the six rice cooking pots (Tables 5.2 and 5.3) match closely those from the raw Kalinga rice. Figure 5.2 shows that the ratios of 16:0, 18:0, and 18:1 for the rice cooking pots cluster around the value for rice. In all cases, the 18:0/16:0 value is much less than the 18:1/16:0 value and the signature fatty acid, 14:0, is found in all pots except H92 Exp7. Interestingly, 12:0 is found, sometimes in quite high proportions, in four of the rice cooking pots. This could either be a common fatty acid in a Kalinga rice variety not analyzed in our study (i.e., only one of four Kalinga rice varieties was analyzed), or 12:0 could be a breakdown product of 18:2. Regardless, the general pattern of the fatty acid profiles of the raw rice and the Kalinga rice cooking pots match reasonably well.

Vegetable/Meat Pots

The *oppaya*, vegetable/meat cooking pots, are used to cook everything in the Kalinga diet that is not rice (even a special form of rice can be cooked

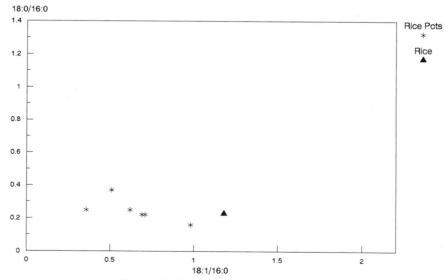

Figure 5.2. Fatty acid ratios (rice, rice pots).

in an *oppaya*). One would expect, therefore, that the fatty acid profiles would be variable and complex; this is indeed the case (Table 5.2). The 18:0, 16:0 ratio ranges from 0.38 to 1.32 and 18:1/16:0 goes from a low of 0.06 to 1.07 (see Table 5.3).

If the vegetable/meat pots are looked at as a group, it is apparent that none of them was used used to cook rice. In Figure 5.3, the vegetable and meat pots cluster within the range of the meat and vegetables in an area that is clearly separate from the rice cooking pots (Figure 5.4).

Only one pot (H99 P12) has definite evidence that it was used to cook meat. The residue from this vessel has a steroid (see Table 5.2) that clearly links it to meat. But based upon the fatty acid ratios (see Table 5.3), it also appears that this pot was used to cook vegetables; only vegetables have such a low 18:1, 16:0 ratio. One other vessel (H42 P7) has 16:0, 18:0, and 18:1 ratios that match with meat (see Table 5.3). Saturated fats are found in high percentages in two vessels (H92 EXP3 and H92 EXP1), but other aspects of their fatty acid profile do not match meat. This may be an example of what can happen if both meat and vegetables are regularly cooked.

As expected, the fatty acid profiles for the vegetable/meat pots are complex. None of the pottery residues could be linked to a specific

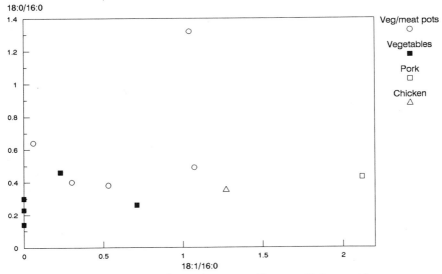

Figure 5.3. Fatty acid ratios (meat, vegetables, vegetable/meat pots).

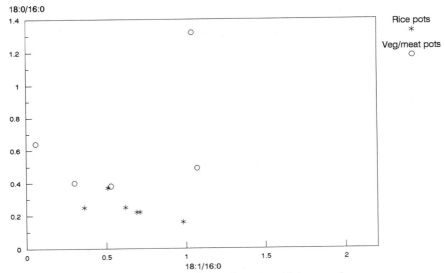

Figure 5.4. Fatty acid ratios (rice, vegetable/meat pots).

vegetable, but there is evidence in four of the five samples that suggests that they were used to cook *some* vegetable besides rice. Residue from one vessel yielded a steroid and provides strong evidence that it was used to cook meat. Three other pots have evidence they were used to cook meat, but in neither case could the species be identified. So, despite the complexity of the fatty acid data, some information is available for what was cooked in the vegetable/meat cooking pots.

Several things were learned from the residue analysis applied to the ethnographic collection. First, the techniques used in this study are successful in separating and identifying fatty acids. In general, unambiguous mass spectra were obtained for nearly all the raw foods, and the residues were taken from the pots. Second, despite some breakdown of fatty acids during cooking or by oxidation, clear links could be made between what was boiled in the vessel and the resultant fatty acid residue. This is particularly true for rice cooking pots. Finally, determining what was cooked in a particular pot is problematic. Certainly, the best cases for a link between residue and food can be made with vessels used to cook one item, as is the case for rice pots. Less clear links can be made between plant or animal species and the fatty acid residue when the pots were used to cook more than one item. This is clearly illustrated by the vegetable/meat pots. Fatty acids in the walls of vegetable/meat pots are the result of many cooking episodes with different items. The ratios of fatty acids are less useful in such cases, and individual species could only be determined if signature fatty acids were present. In the Kalinga case, it could be determined that the vegetable/meat pots were used to cook a variety of items (besides rice), and conclusive evidence for meat cooking was found in one vessel.

Archaeological Sherds

Ten Kalinga archaeological sherds were analyzed, and all have fatty acids (Tables 5.2 and 5.3). This suggests that they were used to cook or store organic material. The problem is that there is evidence that the fatty acids in the sherds have decomposed. One of these processes, which forms a substance known as adipocere (discussed later), results in greater quantities of 16:0 and losses of other less stable fatty acids. Although the process is not complete (for example, 18:1 is present in some samples), it does appear to have changed the ratios of the major fatty acids. Most Kalinga sherds have 18:0/16:0 and 18:1/16:0 values less than 0.50, but similar ratios for the cooking pots often exceed 0.50. Moreover, only one Kalinga sherd had a 18:1/16:0 value greater than the ratio of 16:0/18:0, a pattern found in 8 of the 11 cooking pots (rice and vegetable/meat cooking combined).

There is no reason to believe that Kalinga pottery use or diet has changed in ways that would create the differences between the fatty acid profiles of the sherds and contemporary pots. Moreover, the research by Rottlander (1990:40), Heron et al. (1991b), and Hill et al. (1985) suggests that fats in the pottery matrix are rarely contaminated by the surrounding soil. The sherds seem to have excessive amounts of 16:0 at the expense of the other fatty acids, suggesting that the adipocere transition has indeed occurred.

Fatty Acid Decomposition

Two processes are most responsible for the decomposition of fatty acids: oxidation and hydrolysis. Soon after an organism dies, oxidation of its fat begins. Oxidation is a process whereby the fats, primarily unsaturated fats, are transformed into aldehydes and ketones (Evans 1963:6). The Kalinga sherds appeared to have undergone oxidation; the overall amount of fatty acids had been reduced, and unsaturated fatty acids were not as frequently found as in the currently used cooking vessels.

Fatty acids that survive oxidation can undergo hydrolysis. Instead of breaking down the fatty acids, as in oxidation, hydrolysis transforms the acids into a matter called adipocere. Morgan et al. (1973) attributes the term *adipocere* to Fourcroy (1790) who was describing the material that was found in the exhumation of human remains from a Paris cemetery. Adipocere is "a waxy material formed from animal [or any] fat by microbiological action, during burial in wet, anaerobic conditions" (Thorton et al. 1970:20). This substance can be distinguished because it is composed primarily of saturated fatty acids (mostly 16:0). The problem for those who are interested in characterizing fats that have been long buried in the soil is that the transformation to adipocere appears to occur with any organic material. Matter as different as human fat and olive oil after decomposition become dominated by 16:0 (Thorton et al. 1970). Moreover, Morgan et al. (1973) found that the ratios of fatty acids can completely change over time. In their experiment, the 16:0/18:0 figure for fresh mutton fat is 0.60, and the ratio for 16:0/18:1 is 0.53. After 430 days, the ratios were drastically changed to 3.28 and 9.85, respectively (Morgan et al. 1973:10). Not only did the amount of each fatty acid change, but the relative proportions of the fatty acids were also altered. After 430 days, mutton could not be identified based on fatty acids.

Two conditions that favor adipocere formation are moisture and the lack of oxygen (Evans 1963:48). As discussed earlier, it appears that the Kalinga sherds were also subject to adipocere formation because of the dominance of 16:0 and the changes that occurred in fatty acid ratios. Some recent studies, however, suggest that there are situations in which hydrolysis may not be complete after long periods and that it is possible to link fatty acids with specific plant or animal species. Even Morgan, who was one of the first to voice a word of caution regarding fatty acid preservation, found that the process of adipocere formation in a Thule midden was not complete after 1,000 years (Morgan et al. 1984). Although Morgan and his colleagues found that the relatively unstable polyunsaturated fatty acids were absent, probably removed by oxidation, they were still able to make some general correlations between the fatty acids from a midden and several animal species.

Even stronger claims about the stability of fatty acids have been made by some Japanese researchers. For example, Nakano (1989b) has identified the fatty acids from fish deposited 100,000 years ago. His experiments have shown that fatty acids start to decompose after 1 week and that most of the changes occur within the first 4 months after burial (Nakano 1989a). After 4 years of burial, the amount of fatty acid matter has been greatly reduced, but the important finding by Nakano (1989a:115-116) is that the relative proportions of the fatty acids remain the same. This suggests that there are some conditions of archaeological deposition that can in fact protect the fatty acids and keep them from undergoing transformations by oxidation or hydrolysis.

In the sample of fatty acids extracted from an archaeological sherd, it is possible to infer whether oxidation and hydrolysis had occurred—as was done with the Kalinga pottery. A lack of unsaturated fats suggests that oxidation has broken down some of the material into nonfatty acid constituents. A fatty acid profile dominated by saturated fats, however, needs to be interpreted with caution because many meats do not have significant amounts of unsaturated fat.

One would know that hydrolysis had occurred if adipocere is present. This substance can be identified by the presence of only a few of the stable fatty acids and by the domination of 16:0 (see Deal and Silk 1988). The fatty acid profiles from the Kalinga archaeological sherds suggest that both oxidation and hydrolysis had occurred. But the research suggests that there are conditions where fatty acids will be preserved. In fact, the most extreme environmental situations (permanently wet or dry) are probably the best conditions for fatty acid preservation (Rottlander 1990).

Marchbanks (1989:116) has found that the problem of oxidation can be avoided by taking samples 1 mm below the interior surface. He suggests that by removing the upper 1 mm of the pottery surface, the oxidized fatty acids are not included in the sample and that other forms of contamination, from the soil or from handling the sherds, are also avoided. A number of polyunsaturated fats are represented in sherds analyzed by Marchbanks, suggesting that the interior surface of the pottery wall is indeed protected from oxidation. These sherds also appear to contain little adipocere, suggesting that the area sampled, 1 mm below the surface, provided a place that was not favorable for adipocere formation.

The sampling strategy employed by Marchbanks (1989) avoided some of the problems of fatty acid decomposition. Oxidation may have been avoided by sampling 1 mm below the surface; the exterior surface may have served to protect the fatty acids that are absorbed into the vessel wall. It is not clear, however, why fatty acids in his sample show little sign of adipocere. Most pottery in pre-Columbian North America is porous and permeable, easily permitting the absorption of water. Apparently, moisture did not penetrate into the interior surfaces of the pottery allowing for the formation of adipocere. Evans (1963) found, in an examination of the chemistry of human flesh decomposition, that the formation of adipocere is subject to microenvironmental conditions. He reports a mass grave where some bodies had great amounts of adipocere and others did not. In pottery, microenvironmental conditions should also govern adipocere formation.

DISCUSSION AND SUMMARY

In the introduction to this chapter, I suggested that two requirements must be met before any residue analysis becomes widely employed by archaeologists. The first requirement was that the technique must be accurate. This is the first study to use exclusively an ethnographic pottery sample for which there is accurate data on vessel use. The analysis demonstrated that fatty acids absorbed in Kalinga pottery under real cooking conditions could be linked to food groups or in some cases specific plants or animals. Rice cooking vessels could be clearly discriminated from vegetable/meat cooking pots. However, determining what had been cooked in each vegetable/meat pot was found to be more problematic. Certainly, it can be said that a variety of items were boiled in the pots, and there is evidence that several pots were used to cook meat, but the specific animal species could not be differentiated on the basis of fatty acid profiles. But the level of specificity in the identification of plants or animals from fatty acids must be determined on a case-by-case basis. Many of the items cooked in the vegetable/meat pots have, by chance, similar fatty acid profiles. It is possible that in other study areas the foods stored or cooked in ceramic pots may have very different fatty acids. The level of discrimination in any one fatty acid analysis will be variable. Certainly, larger sample sizes may be necessary in the initial investigation of fatty acids within a pottery assemblage.

The accuracy and reliability of a fatty acid analysis in archaeology is most jeopardized by processes of fatty acid decomposition. It was discussed how oxidation can reduce the overall amount of fatty acids in pottery and totally break down some of the unsaturated fats. Moreover, the fatty acids that survive oxidation can be subject to hydrolysis under appropriate environmental conditions. Hydrolysis can lead to the formation of adipocere and make it impossible to link fatty acids to their source. Luckily, in the analysis of fatty acids, it is possible to identify whether either of these decomposition processes have altered the sample, and we are beginning to understand which environments least affect fats absorbed into the vessel (Rottlander 1990). Moreover, Marchbanks (1989) has shown that some of the contaminated or decomposed fatty acids can be avoided by extracting the sample well below the pottery surface. This seems particularly appropriate for avoiding the oxidized fatty acids, but it is still unclear whether this technique can avoid the fatty acids subject to hydrolysis.

The second requirement suggested in the introduction of this chapter is that any residue technique must be presented in a way that will make it possible for archaeologists to integrate it into their research pursuits. It was found, when developing the methods used in this study, that in many cases (with exceptions) it is difficult to replicate the specific procedures from the published reports of other researchers. Every effort was made here to provide the amount of detail necessary for anyone to extract and analyze fatty acids. Gas chromatography/ mass spectrometry facilities can be found on most college campuses and the cost per sample is not great. The GC/MS can perform a computer library search of fatty acids and identify the fats and other chemicals in a sample.

Recommendations for Future Research

Though fatty acid analysis can now be done accurately and practically, I concur with Rottlander (1990:40) that identifying the contents of vessels with remnant fats is "still a difficult procedure." Two factors lead me to this conclusion. First, there is not enough basic fatty acid chemistry. Though the GC/MS can provide accurate estimates of the fatty acid content of a sample, the archaeologist is still left with the task of matching these data to the fatty acid profiles of known food groups. Because there is not a reference book of fats in plants in animals, the researcher usually must analyze a sample of foods as a comparative sample. For fatty acid analysis to become commonplace, there is a need for a library of plant and animal fatty acid compositions that could be at the disposal of any archaeologist (cf. Rottlander 1990). I suggest that researchers in this area share their raw data to build a common reference library of plant and animal fatty acids. Such a library would reduce the cost of research and facilitate the use of fatty acid studies in archaeology. Moreover, including the analysis of sterols in the routine study of organic residue (cf. Heron *et al.* 1991a) will aid in the discrimination of individual plant or animal species.

The second reason that fatty acid analysis is "still a difficult procedure" is that there is still much to be learned about fatty acid preservation. My analysis of Kalinga midden sherds demonstrated clearly that fats do not always preserve in a state that can be useful. But the analysis also showed that erroneous conclusions can usually be avoided because decomposition products can be identified. Though we now know that permanently wet or dry conditions are probably best for fatty acid preservation (Rottlander 1990), the process is subject to microenvironmental conditions and one cannot, at this point, predict whether fats will be preserved in the vessel matrix. A vessel wall can act in some cases, as a tomb for the preservation of fats despite deleterious environmental conditions. Clearly, more experiments are necessary.

Chapter **6**

Use Alteration: Surface Attrition

Analyses of prehistoric lithic assemblages often employ use-wear traces to make inferences about tool technofunction. It is just recently, however, that ceramic use-wear (referred to here as surface attrition) has received some attention. This is appropriate because ceramic surface attrition can, potentially, provide information about use behavior at the same level of specificity as lithic use-wear studies. We lack only the appropriate theoretical and methodological framework to put the analysis of ceramic surface attrition in a position similar to lithic use-wear studies.

In this chapter, ceramic surface attrition is first defined, and then an analysis of use attrition is performed on the Kalinga pottery. Attrition on Kalinga cooking vessels is found on nine different regions of the pots, and the traces in each area are linked to specific pottery use activities. The attrition patterns on the rice and vegetable/meat cooking vessels are then contrasted to demonstrate the relationship between ceramic surface attrition and broad pottery use categories. I take the reader through a rather detailed discussion of surface attrition to demonstrate the direct link between activity and trace. This analysis illustrates that by understanding several principles regarding the relationship between a ceramic surface and abrader, specific activities of pottery use can be inferred. This builds on the work of Schiffer and Skibo (1989) by providing examples of the interaction between the pottery surface and the use activity. Using a similar strategy, prehistorians will be able to link surface attrition to specific pottery use activities.

CERAMIC SURFACE ATTRITION DEFINED

Ceramic surface attrition is defined simply as the removal or deformation of ceramic surfaces. The framework presented in Chapter 4 (see also Table 3.1) points out that ceramic alteration can occur in a variety of use and nonuse contexts. Postdepositional processes such as fluvial and aeolian action or freeze-thaw processes can cause abrasion of pottery surfaces (for a discussion of these and other processes, see Schiffer 1987:158-162). Surface attrition related to use includes various forms of abrasive and nonabrasive processes caused during cooking, cleaning, and storing of pots. This is why I use the rather clumsy term of *ceramic surface attrition,* instead of *ceramic abrasion* or *ceramic wear.* The latter two terms do not include all forms of surface modification that pertain to pottery use alteration.

Nonabrasive forms of ceramic use attrition include processes such as salt erosion (cf. O'Brien 1990), common on water storage vessels, or spalling of the surface of cooking vessels as they are placed over heat. Certainly, abrasion is the principal form of use attrition, and it has already been the focus of case studies (e.g., Bray 1982; Griffiths 1978; Hally 1983a; Henrickson 1990; Jones 1989) and a theoretical framework (Schiffer and Skibo 1989), but use attrition not caused by an abrasive process can create informative traces that need to be considered in any study of use alteration.

Schiffer and Skibo (1989:101-102) define an abrasion as a "trace that was formed by removal or deformation of material on a ceramic's surface by mechanical contact, specifically, the sliding, scraping, or, in some cases, striking action of an abrader (i.e., a particle, object, or surface)." Nonabrasive use attrition is, therefore, any trace that occurred because of use but that did not involve mechanical action. The most common examples involve the expansion of a substance absorbed inside the ceramic body; in salt erosion the expansion during the formation of salt crystals causes the damage, and in "steam blowing" the rapid escape of vaporized water can cause spalling. In many cases one would expect that ceramic surfaces could be weakened by salt erosion and steam blowing and become more susceptible to various attritional processes.

A number of other processes can also render a ceramic surface more susceptible to ceramic abrasion. The presence of moisture can make ceramics abrade at higher rates (Skibo and Schiffer 1987), and certainly thermal stress caused by repeated heating and cooling would promote greater susceptibility to all forms of abrasion.

At this point, it is instructive to distinguish a ceramic surface from a pottery surface. A ceramic surface is simply fired paste that includes clay and various forms of nonclay substances such as sand or some organic matter. A pottery surface is, however, not only fired clay and temper but also any substance added by the potter as surface treatment or any matter that adheres to the surface as a result of use or through processes in the depositional environment. Thus, a pottery use-attrition study must include traces on the ceramic surface and on various surface treatments, such as resins, or material that adheres to the surface as a result of use, such as soot. Certainly this can complicate an analysis, but it also provides other forms of use information. For example, some use activities do not abrade the ceramic but can abrade a softer surface treatment such as resin (there is evidence for this on the Kalinga pots). Nonetheless, attrition of the ceramic surface will more often be the trace important in a use-alteration study. Matter adhering to a pottery surface, even surface treatments such as resins, will seldom survive in the depositional environment, and use-attrition traces on this material will not be available for study. In addition, myriad forms of matter can adhere to a pottery surface, and so a complete description of attrition of these surfaces would be impossible. It is for these reasons that I concentrate on ceramic attrition. The pottery use-alteration analyst must evaluate attrition of these nonceramic surfaces on a case-by-case basis and certainly be aware that the surface of a pot while in use may have been covered by a material not now visible on the archaeological specimen.

I now discuss the processes involved in abrasive and nonabrasive use attrition. Pottery use abrasion is the primary agent of use attrition, and more effort is given to describing this process. This chapter concludes with an analysis of Kalinga pottery use attrition.

Use Attrition—Abrasive Processes

As mentioned in Chapter 3, abrasion studies of prehistoric ceramics have not to date been successful in linking specific abrasive traces to pottery use activities. Although some studies have demonstrated that ceramic abrasion can cause different types of traces and that there is often intraassemblage variability in ceramic abrasion (e.g., Bray 1982; Griffiths 1978; Hally 1983a; Jones 1989), there has been little success in linking an abrasive trace to a particular activity. Only Griffiths (1978), in an analysis of lead-glazed historic ceramics, has been able to make distinctions in use abrasion and attribute them to a particular abrader. She contrasted scratches on soup and dinner plates and found that knives, spoons, and forks leave distinct traces. Moreover, specific abrasive patterns on the exterior bases and rims provided information on how the ceramics were stored and used.

Although the study by Griffiths has not been widely employed (even on lead-glazed ceramics), it is important research because it demonstrates the potential of a systematic use-abrasion analysis. She was able to make a number of inferences about ceramic use, including use life, that would be unobtainable by traditional ceramic analyses. Although this work is a significant contribution to use-alteration studies, the specific findings cannot be applied directly in the study of abrasion of low-fired prehistoric ceramics. Low-fired, heterogeneous ceramic bodies abrade differently from eighteenth-century glazed tableware; moreover, a unique set of behaviors is associated with pottery use in a more traditional context.

To investigate and understand ceramic abrasive processes, Schiffer and Skibo (1989) suggest dividing the analysis into three separate areas of inquiry: characteristics of the ceramic, characteristics of the abrader, and the nature of the ceramic-abrader contact. Examples of how these characteristics affect abrasion are provided in the analysis of Kalinga pottery, but at this time the principal components of each is reviewed briefly.

Characteristics of the Ceramic

The first of six important characteristics of the ceramic (Schiffer and Skibo 1989:105-108) is strength of the fired paste. Both the rate and nature of abrasion are determined by strength of the ceramic body, which can be controlled in large degree by the potter. A primary determinant of ceramic strength and its resistance to abrasion is firing temperature (see Skibo *et al.* 1989a; Vaz Pinto *et al.* 1987). The second factor is the nature of the ceramic surface, especially the presence of pores, cracks, and voids. Certainly, any time the ceramic topography has voids it becomes more susceptible to abrasion.

The third, fourth, and fifth characteristics relate to the temper particles. The hardness of temper, in addition to size, quantity, distribution, and orientation, can all influence ceramic abrasion. The final characteristic is the shape of the ceramic piece and nature of the surface (for a full discussion, see Schiffer and Skibo 1989).

To these six characteristics I add the "nature of the pottery surface."

As discussed, pottery abrasion is not just confined to the ceramic surfaces; surface treatments applied in manufacture and various surface coatings acquired during use and in the depositional environment will not only abrade and provide use information but also serve to protect the ceramic surface.

Characteristics of the Abrader

Schiffer and Skibo (1989:108-111) also discuss how characteristics of the abrader, such as hardness, shape, and size, can affect the overall abrasion process. Certainly, hardness of the abrader in relation to the ceramic determines in part the rate of abrasion and also characteristics of the abrasive trace. One can easily envision the different forms of abrasive marks made by stirring the contents of a pot with a metal, wood, and ceramic ladle. Likewise, abraders of different shape and size will impart different abrasive traces. For example, it has been demonstrated that abraders that have a diameter less than the distance between temper particles will create distinctive types of abrasion (e.g., pedestalled temper). Furthermore, if an abrader had a spherical shape, one would expect the abrasive trace to be much different from one caused by an angular abrader.

Nature of the Ceramic–Abrader Contact

A number of factors are involved in the interaction between abrader and ceramic that affect the rate and traces of abrasion (Schiffer and Skibo 1989:111-113). Abrasion requires, typically, movement in either the abrader, ceramic, or both. The directionality, velocity, and the rate of contact of this relative motion determine the nature of abrasive traces. However, several factors can make the relationship between ceramic and abrader more complicated. For example, at any one spot on a ceramic vessel numerous abraders may have made contact. In some cases all or many of the traces of the abrasions may be present, but in others one abrasive trace may obliterate the others. A second complicating factor is when the abrasive situation consists of the ceramic, abrader, and a substrate. An example of this would be washing a pot with sand; the hand moving over the pot is the substrate, and sand is the abrader. A final factor is the presence of liquid; in general, liquid will increase the rate of abrasion and in some cases create traces different than those produced by similar forms of abrasion in the absence of liquid (see Skibo and Schiffer 1987).

Use Attrition—Nonabrasive Processes

There are two common forms of nonabrasive use attrition. The first is salt erosion, a common form of attrition on the surface of permeable water vessels. O'Brien (1990) has carried out experiments in salt erosion. Briefly, salt erosion takes place as water permeates the wall of a pot and then evaporates leaving a residue of salt. The salts can then crystallize and if there is not enough pore volume for the growth of crystals, the exterior ceramic surface will usually exfoliate.

A second form of nonabrasive use attrition is thermal spalling. This is similar to the process that creates spalls on insufficiently dried pottery during firing (Rye 1981:114). Basically, thermal spalling is caused by vaporization of water that has been absorbed in the vessel wall. The rapid escape of water vapor usually creates a cone-shaped spall. Damage caused by both thermal spalling and salt erosion is greatly influenced by the characteristics of the ceramic, just as abrasive forms of surface attrition. Both thermal spalling and salt erosion require that the pottery surface be permeable to water. Although virtually all open-fired ceramics are permeable, there are several ways to reduce permeability and thus susceptibility to processes such as salt erosion and thermal spalling.

Permeability can be controlled primarily with surface treatments (Rice 1987:230-232). Schiffer (1990) demonstrates that interior and exterior surface treatments can control liquid permeability even to the point of completely stopping the flow of moisture. One would anticipate that a pottery surface with lower permeability and lower density than the interior body would be very susceptible to attrition caused by thermal spalls.

Susceptibility to ceramic spalling is also controlled by ceramic strength. Because firing temperature has the greatest influence on pottery strength (Skibo *et al.* 1989a), higher fired vessels are less likely to be damaged by salt erosion (see O'Brien 1990) and thermal spalling.

KALINGA POTTERY USE ATTRITION

Attrition on Kalinga pots is confined to nine areas. In this section, each area is first described and then linked to a specific use. The general use-attrition patterns for rice and vegetable/meat cooking vessels are described and contrasted. In this discussion, there is a distinct lack of quantitative analysis. It may be appropriate in other use-attrition studies, but an effort was made to describe the attritional patterns in very robust terms. The objective of a pottery use-attrition study is to determine the general pattern of use traces and link them to various activities. Patterned use of pottery can and does leave very distinct and easily recognizable attritional traces. These can be discerned and described, especially in the Kalinga case, without resort to much quantification. All rice and vegetable/meat cooking pots that have been used enough times to have surface attrition exhibit—without exception—a consistent pattern of surface attrition.

Use-Attrition Terms

There are two broad categories of use-attrition traces: marks and patches (Schiffer 1989:194-196). A mark, the result of a single attritional event, is the lowest-level use-attrition trace, and it may take the from of a scratch, pit, chip, or nick. Factors such as the direction of motion, angle of contact, shape of abrader, and force applied are important in the formation of an attritional mark.

"Use activity," in the context of this study, refers to an action that was repeated during the normal use of pottery vessels. Different sets of activities are associated with different vessel uses and different vessel types. Certainly, individual acts can leave use traces, but it is the typical routine of pottery use that can leave the distinctive use-alteration patterns that are of interest here.

As a use activity is repeated, an attritional patch may form. A patch is often the result of multiple attritional marks, but in many cases individual marks cannot be identified. It is possible that some use activities will not form distinguishable marks, as in the contact between the human hand and ceramic, but if that contact is repeated enough times, a distinctive patch may form. Patches may also have distinct zones consisting of a center and periphery (Schiffer 1989:195). Individual marks may not be visible in the center, which can consist of hundreds of marks, but traces of marks might be present on the periphery. Although a patch could lose the evidence of individual marks, distinctive features of the patch, such as size, location, and characteristics of the pottery surface, can still provide information on use behavior.

Characteristics of the Pottery Surface

In order to characterize use attrition, it is necessary to describe the surface of Kalinga vessels. The pottery surface, as described, includes both the ceramic and the surface matter that was acquired after vessel firing. The clay used to manufacture Kalinga pottery (from the villages of Dangtalan and Dalupa) is composed primarily of montmorillonite and a relatively large amount of nonclay particles (Aronson *et al.* n.d.). As already noted, the nonclay particles are found naturally in the clay, and no other temper is added during vessel manufacture (Longacre 1981). The Kalinga clay has a relatively high percentage of nonplastics, which helps to counter the high shrinkage of montmorillonite clay, and the individual particles include rounded quartz grains (up to 3.5-4.0 mm in diameter), angular biotite mica (up to 2-3 mm), and a number of siliceous minerals (up to 3 mm) (Aronson *et al.* n.d.).

Kalinga pottery is very low fired. Firings usually last about 20 minutes, and the temperature of the open-air fire rarely exceeds 700° C. This creates a ceramic body with low overall impact strength and abrasion resistance. Probably to compensate for the low firing temperature, the potter applies resin to the interior and exterior lip and rim of cooking pots and usually to the interior and exterior of water storage vessels (although some potters have now stopped putting the exterior resin on the water storage pots). The resin, applied while the vessel is still hot after firing, creates a surface with higher abrasion resistance and with a much lower permeability (though the pots are not completely impermeable). Although the layer of resin acts as a barrier to use attrition, many informative traces can be preserved on the resin. Nonetheless, the ceramic surface on the interior of the pots eventually becomes exposed as the pot is used (Kobayashi n.d.).

The Kalinga pots are polished on both the interior and exterior surfaces (for further details of manufacture, see Chapter 4 and Longacre 1981). The resultant pottery surfaces, after firing, are quite smooth to the touch. Temper particles do not protrude from the vessel wall, though fine sand particles are visible on the surface.

After several uses, cooking vessel exteriors usually become completely covered with soot from the smoke of the fire. This layer of carbon can become quite thick and can even begin to chip off after many uses. Soot can also impede attrition of the ceramic, but on Kalinga pots the attritional patches almost always extend to the ceramic surface. In most of these cases, attrition of soot provides additional information but does not detract from evidence of attrition on the ceramic itself.

Deposits of carbonized material can also occur on the interior of

Kalinga cooking vessels. These result mainly from the burning and carbonization of food. This layer, however, is never thick and does not influence significantly attrition of interior surfaces. Of course, interior and exterior carbonization is itself an informative use alteration trace and is discussed in more detail in Chapter 7.

Resin and carbon deposited on the surface of Kalinga pottery are important to the study of use attrition in two ways. First, they can act as a barrier between the use activity and the ceramic surface; in some cases such a barrier could protect the surface from attrition. After many uses, however, neither the resin nor the carbon deposits completely protect the ceramic surface.

Second, carbon deposits and resin can provide additional sources of attritional data. Neither resin nor carbon deposits abrade like pottery—both are generally softer and more prone to abrasion. Evidence of use that would not be abrasive enough to remove ceramic material can be encoded in the surfaces of resin or soot. One problem is the preservation of many organic surface treatments; resin was only occasionally seen on the Kalinga sherds excavated in Puapo. Carbon deposits, however, usually survive, and should be another source of information for a use-attrition study.

Use Attrition of Kalinga Pots

Kalinga cooking pots have a unique set of use-attrition traces. In the discussion that follows, the use-attrition marks and patches on each cooking vessel are described and then matched to the use activity responsible for creating that trace (see Chapter 4 for a general discussion of Kalinga pottery use). Each use activity is described in terms of characteristics of the abrader and the abrader-pottery surface contact. Nine different points on the interior and exterior of Kalinga cooking pots reveal evidence of use. Terminology to locate these points on the jars (see Figure 6.1) has been adapted from Griffiths (1978:70-71).

The vegetable/meat cooking pots (*oppaya*) and rice cooking pots (*ittoyom*) (Figure 6.2) are discussed together because they share many use-attrition traces. But the vegetable/meat and rice cooking pots are also associated with a set of distinctive use activities and use-attrition traces and thus a comparison of the two is instructive.

1. *Exterior base* (Figure 6.1). All cooking vessels have a circular abrasive patch, about 3 to 6 cm in diameter, that corresponds to an area

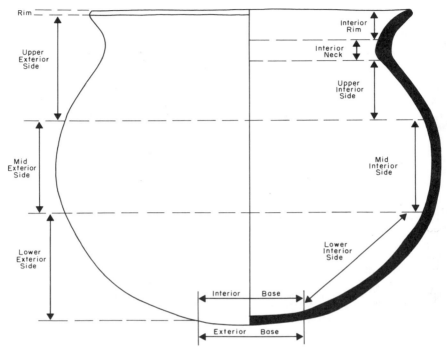

Figure 6.1. Vessel location terminology.

that is slightly larger than the basal portion of the pot that is in contact with the ground while the vessel is in an upright position. The use activity that directly affects the exterior base consists of (1) setting the pot down on the hearth soil, bamboo floor, ground surface, or cement near the water source; (2) putting the pot down and at times tipping and

Figure 6.2. Kalinga cooking pots.

rotating the full pot during serving while it rests on a bamboo pot rest, the hearth soil, or the bamboo floor; (3) dragging the pot (empty or full) along the hearth soil or bamboo floor; (4) rotating the rice cooking pots on a bed of coals while the pot is in the third stage of cooking; and (5) rubbing the pot during washing with one's hand, and sometimes with sand, leaves, rice chaff, a wet cloth, or charcoal.

The placement and morphology of the abrasive patch on the exterior base provide information about use activity. Basal attrition (in this case abrasion) suggests that the vessel was in contact with an abrader while in an upright position. In the heavily used pots, the basal abrasion has two separate regions, the center and periphery. The center, usually only including the area that comes in contact with the ground, often has the original surface completely removed. Pits and pedestalled temper are the most common abrasive traces. The periphery is composed of individual marks, usually pits, scratches, and gouges. The center of the patch is the area most often in contact with an abrader during use, whereas the periphery is only abraded if the vessel is tipped slightly during contact with the ground surface. On a vessel used less frequently, only the center has abrasive marks, which are similar to the marks on the periphery of heavily used vessels. Individual marks, therefore, are formed during contact with the ground surface, and the accumulation of these marks over time will remove the surface in the center region. The primary marks on the exterior base are pits (including nicks and gouges), pedestalled temper, and scratches. Each of these traces is now discussed in turn.

Pits (Figure 6.3) are caused by the removal of temper, especially after it has been pedestalled, and by small chips, nicks, and gouges from single impacts of an abrader. The latter appears to be the primary agent responsible for the pits on the exterior base of the cooking vessels. Individual marks in the form of nicks or gouges occur frequently in this region, often in the absence of pedestalled temper. A mark of this type is likely caused by a forceful contact from roughly a 90° angle with a small abrader that is harder than the ceramic. The use activity most likely responsible for this mark is setting down a full pot on the hearth soil that consists of compact earth. When a vessel is set down, sand particles create gouges in the pottery surface. The placement of the pots on the ground or on rough cement at the water sources could also create pitting, but the pots are usually not full at this time, and the contact would not be as forceful.

Figure 6.3. Pits on the exterior base (length of the frame is approximately 13 mm).

Pedestalled temper (Figure 6.4) is created by gentle abrasion by material that has a diameter less than the distance between temper particles (Skibo 1987). The contact between abrader and ceramic must be such that ceramic material is removed around individual temper particles. Pedestalled temper occurs primarily in the center of the patch where the original surface is not intact. Contact with the hearth soil, which has a granular texture, is most likely responsible for creating this trace. The use activity that creates pedestalled temper is the turning and tipping of the pot (often during serving) on the hearth soil.

Scratches (Figure 6.5) are oriented in all directions, although there seems to be a tendency, particularly on vegetable/meat cooking pots, for scratches to travel from the center of the patch to the perimeter. The scratches imply that the pot was moved over a surface that consisted of small particles harder than the pottery surface. The use activity that is most responsible for creation of scratches is the dragging of the pot along the hearth soil. In addition, the pot is slid on its base for a short distance as it is picked up.

In summary, there is evidence that the cooking vessels had contact with a small abrader in three types of situations: (1) forceful impact at a 90° angle, (2) gentle abrasive contact, and (3) a contact that involved

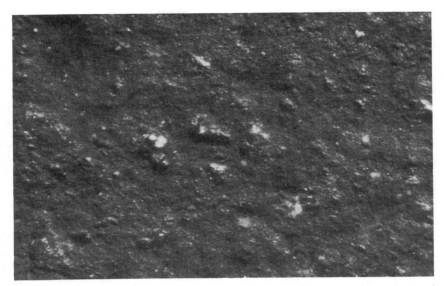

Figure 6.4. Pedestalled temper on the exterior base (length of the frame is approximately 3 mm).

movement. Observations of pottery use suggest that these abrasive situations consist of the manipulation of the pot on the hearth soil before and after it is on the fire. In this case, no differences could be seen in use attrition between the exterior base of the vegetable/meat and rice cooking pots.

There is, however, one use activity that affects the exterior base that is very different for the rice cooking pots. In the third stage of cooking, the pots are set next to the fire on a bed of coals and rotated several times over a 10- to 20-minute period. No evidence of this activity is found on the exterior bases of the rice cooking pots. But use attrition on other parts of the vessel, in addition to the carbon deposits discussed in Chapter 7, provide evidence for this activity.

Several other use activities that affect the exterior base leave no trace. The pots are often placed, then tipped and turned on a rattan ring after they are taken off the fire, but there is no evidence for this on the base. Both rice and vegetable/meat cooking pots are also set down on the split-bamboo kitchen floor either while the pots are being filled or food is being served, but there are no traces of this activity. Finally, there are none of the fine scratches (discussed later) created by washing and found on the rest of the vessel exterior. There are two reasons for the lack of fine washing scratches: (1) There is none of the glossy soot on the base,

Figure 6.5. Scratch on the exterior base (length of frame is approximately 7 mm).

which abrades easily and records the fine scratches; and (2) the intensive abrasion on the exterior base obliterates the more subtle abrasive traces created during washing.

2. *Lower exterior side* (Figure 6.1). The region is characterized by relatively deep scratches parallel to the rim and by fine scratches oriented in seemingly random directions. The use activities that affect this area are (1) rotating the pot on the ground surface or on cement while washing the interior of the pot; (2) rubbing the pot by hand in combination with sand, leaves, rice chaff, a wet cloth, or charcoal during washing; and (3) contact with the ceramic or stone pot rests in the hearth.

This area along with the midexterior side has the heaviest covering of soot. The lower exterior side is the transition point between a dull/gray layer of soot and a region of dark, glossy soot. The pattern of sooting is discussed in Chapter 7, but it should be mentioned here that the glossy soot deposit can become quite thick and is very good at preserving use-attrition traces. This is one case where the matter adhering to a pottery surface can provide use-attrition information that is not found on the ceramic. The best example of this is the fine scratches that run in seemingly random directions in the glossy sooted area of the lower exterior side (Figure 6.6). These traces are created as the pot is scrubbed,

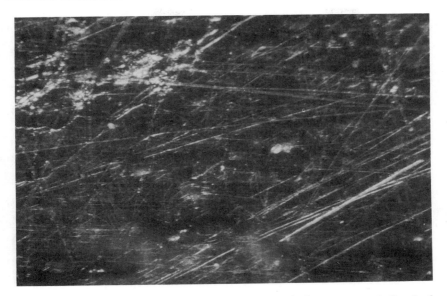

Figure 6.6. Fine scratches that travel in various directions on the lower exterior side (length of frame is approximately 13 mm).

often in a circular motion, with water and sand. The scratches are very fine, and they do not reduce the glossy appearance of the carbon layer.

The most visible use abrasion in this area on the ceramic, though also visible on the carbonized layer, occurs in linear scratches sometimes over a centimeter in length (Figure 6.7). The abrasive patch forms in a band about 2 to 4 cm wide. The scratches are located in unsooted areas or, if the scratching is intense, it penetrates through the soot layer to the ceramic surface.

Several use activity inferences can be made from the scratches. First, the activity involves movement of either the ceramic or abrader, and the abrader surface is less than 1 mm in diameter. Second, the abrader is harder than the ceramic material, and the contact situation involves a relatively great amount of force; in cases in which the surface has been completely abraded, the temper particles are removed instead of being pedestalled. Third, the activity is done repeatedly and consistently. All pots have this band, and the scratches rarely deviate from the linear pattern.

Finally, the abrasive motion usually travels in the same direction. In nearly all of the used pots, the direction of motion that formed the

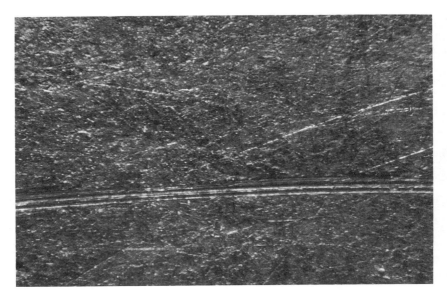

Figure 6.7. Linear scratch on the lower exterior side (length of frame is approximately 7 mm).

scratches could be determined. The best indicator of direction is found on pits that have become eroded from the abrasive action. If the pot is moving and not the abrader, as in this case, the pits are eroded more on the edge that is opposite the direction of the abrasive motion. When the abrasive motion is in one direction only, one lip of the pit is more susceptible to abrasion. A typical pattern is for a pit to be the shape of a horizontal teardrop or to have one side intact and the other eroded.

The unique feature of these scratches is that nearly all pots have been abraded in the same direction. The only exceptions are the pots that come from a household where the person who used and cleaned the pots is left-handed. More will be said about this in the discussion of the midexterior side abrasive patch.

From only the use-attrition traces there is evidence for two types of use activity. The first was applied with a light force, abraded only carbonized areas, and traveled in random directions. The other involved a lot more force, followed a linear path, and traveled in the same direction (with exceptions).

The use activities responsible for these abrasive traces occur during pot washing. The fine scratches are produced as the exterior of the pot is washed, usually by hand scrubbing with a mixture of sand, charcoal, leaves, rice chaff, a wet cloth, or any combination thereof. The scratches are obviously formed by the sand as the washer scrubs the exterior of the pot.

The scratches that travel in a linear direction are created while the interior of the pot is washed (Figure 4.22). It is set on the ground so that the lower exterior side contacts the ground, which consists of either compact soil or rough cement. The pot is usually rotated one complete turn as the interior is washed. Because Kalinga cooking typically involves boiling and the interior of pots usually have very little adhering food residue, washing the inside of pots is not difficult. If the washer is right-handed, the pot is held and rotated with the left hand and scrubbed with the right. The pots are always rotated in a clockwise direction if the washer is right-handed and in a counterclockwise direction if the washer is left-handed.

There are several use activities that do not leave an abrasive trace on the lower exterior side. The most important is the placement of the pot on three supports in the hearth (Figure 6.8). The pot supports are usually ceramic (75 cases), but a number are stone (22 cases), and a few are made of metal (3 cases). The ceramic pot supports are low fired and typically covered with resin, and the stone supports are constructed of an easily hewn local material. Pots are set in the fire, and the supports

Figure 6.8. A rice cooking pot resting on the three ceramic pot supports.

contact the pot on the lower exterior. There are two reasons why there is not an abrasive trace at this point of contact. The first is that a pot is put on pot supports very gently, and there is usually no twisting or turning of the pot after it is in place. The second reason is that the pot supports are covered with a thick layer of soot that serves to cushion the impact with the pot. Moreover, even if there is some subtle trace of the pot support contact, it is likely obliterated by the scratches caused by rotation of the pot on the ground during washing. But the exterior carbon patterns, discussed in Chapter 7, do provide some evidence for how the pot was placed in the hearth.

The only other use activity affecting the lower exterior that does not leave a trace is the scrubbing of the pots when no sand is involved. Charcoal, leaves, rice chaff, a wet rag, or just one's hand are often used to wash the exterior of the pot; this activity does not leave any trace on the lower exterior side.

Rice and vegetable/meat cooking pots could not be distinguished based on abrasion on the lower exterior side. All cooking pots are washed in a similar fashion.

3. *Midexterior side* (Figure 6.1). This region is similar to the lower exterior side in that there are two forms of use attrition: deep linear scratches and fine scratches that travel in seemingly random directions. The difference is that the linear scratches on the midexterior side are more numerous and more deeply incised than those on the lower exterior side. The other important feature of this area is that it is covered entirely by the glossy soot, and it does not have the dull gray soot layer that is characteristic of the lower exterior side.

Some of the activities that impact the midexterior side are (1) scrubbing the pot with one's hand and sand, charcoal, a cloth rag, leaves, rice chaff, or any combination thereof; and (2) rotating the pot on compact soil or rough cement while washing the exterior of the pot (note the lower exterior side contacts the ground while scrubbing the *interior* of the vessel).

The fine scratches in this region cannot be discriminated from those on the lower exterior side. They travel in random directions and are only visible on the carbon layer. This suggests that the abrader is small, relatively hard, and there is not much force in the contact between the abrader and the pottery surface.

Because the same fine scratches also appear on the lower exterior side, it is apparent that a similar abrasive activity affects both regions. This activity is the scrubbing of the vessels by hand as some of the external soot is removed. There is a layer of soot that is easily removed and a layer that is more permanently affixed to the surface (see Chapter 7). The nonpermanent carbon deposit is removed with water and by scrubbing the surface of the pot with sand, charcoal, leaves, and rice chaff. Scrubbing with sand is primarily responsible for causing the scratches.

The linear scratches occur in the carbon layer, but they also penetrate to the ceramic surface. The abrasive trace appears as linear scratches, parallel to the rim, that can travel for over a centimeter (Figure 6.9). The linear scratches are more numerous and more pronounced than those on the lower exterior side.

A number of inferences can be made about the activity that produces the linear scratches. The abrader is small in size but harder than the ceramic material. Because no temper is pedestalled, it implies that the force of contact is relatively great. The action responsible for creating the trace is obviously common and repeated. The linear scratches are more numerous on the midexterior than the lower exterior side suggesting that the abrasive action that creates these traces is repeated more often on the midexterior side. Directionality of motion can also be inferred from the

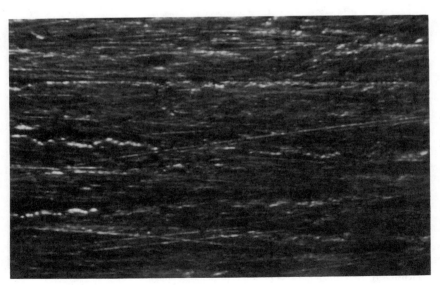

Figure 6.9. Linear scratches, created by washing, on the midexterior side.

pits with erosion on one side (Figure 6.10). On the midexterior side, however, the pots are rotated in a counterclockwise direction, which contrasts with the direction of motion for the linear scratches on the lower exterior side. As Figure 6.11 illustrates, the two bands of linear scratches on the lower and midexterior side, which often merge, were produced by an abrasive action traveling in opposite directions. This pattern of motion is reversed in a household where the pot user and washer is left-handed (compare Figures 6.10 and 6.12).

The use activity responsible for the linear scratches is the rotation of the pot on the ground or on rough cement as the person washes the exterior of the vessel. The linear scratches are more numerous because the washer will rotate the pot more times while scrubbing the exterior. The exterior has a layer of soot (the dull gray layer) that they prefer to wash off, whereas the interior of most vessels is not dirty and does not require much washing. The rotational reversal that creates the attrition on the lower and midexterior side is caused by gripping the pot differently; compare Figure 4.21 to 4.22.

There are also some regular activities that do not leave an abrasive trace in this area. This includes washing of the vessel with leaves, rice

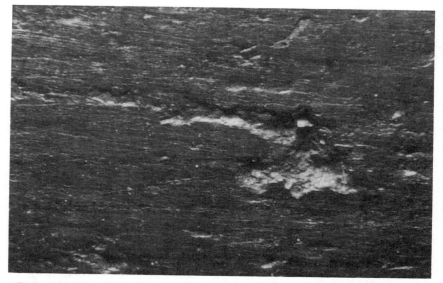

Figure 6.10. Pit eroded more on the left side, indicating the direction of the abrasive motion (length of frame is approximately 13 mm).

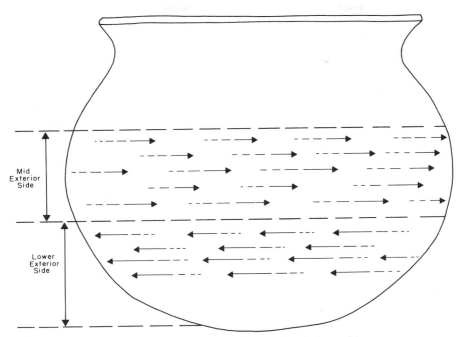

Figure 6.11. Direction of the abrasive action during washing.

chaff, a wet cloth, or charcoal. Because these items are softer than the ceramic material, they create a polish when a scrubbing motion is applied. But this trace is much too subtle and is undoubtedly obliterated by the linear and random scratches.

The washing activity and the traces that result are identical for the rice and vegetable/meat cooking pots. The vessel types could not be distinguished based on midexterior side attrition.

4. *Upper exterior side* (Figure 6.1). The surface of the vessel in this region has a number of unique attributes. The upper exterior side, along with the rim and interior, is covered with a layer of resin. But unlike the interiors, the resin layer on the upper exterior side is rarely penetrated; attrition in this area occurs only on the resin layer, which also has a coating of soot. The upper exterior side also has the *gili*, which is the decorative element on Kalinga pots. The *gili* consists of bands of punctations and incised lines made while the clay is still plastic.

Some of the activities that impact the upper exterior side include

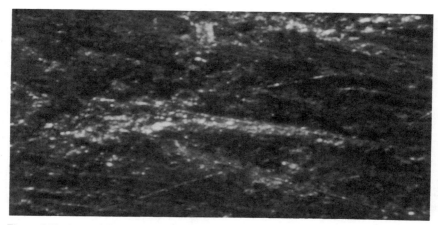

Figure 6.12. Pit eroded more on the right side, indicating that the washer rotated the pot in a reversed direction. The washer in this case is left-handed (length of frame is approximately 13 mm).

(1) lifting the pot off the fire with a rattan pot carrier; (2) carrying the pot (whether full or empty, the pots are usually carried by grasping the rim); and (3) scrubbing the pot by hand and with sand, charcoal, leaves, rice chaff, a wet rag, or any combination thereof.

There is a noticeable break in abrasive traces between the mid- and upper exterior side. The upper exterior side does not contact the ground during washing and does not have the linear scratches characteristic of the mid- and lower exterior side. Abrasion rarely penetrates to the ceramic surface, but the traces on the layer of resin and soot are very instructive. The upper exterior side, in many cases, is very smooth, soft to the touch, and at times reflective of light. The polished surface consists of very fine scratches, not visible with the naked eye, that travel in a direction parallel to the rim (Figure 6.13). The polishing is especially apparent in the neck area up to the outflaring rim. Both the resin and carbon layer have a lower resistance to abrasion than the ceramic surface. The polish in this area suggests that there is contact with a soft abrader; a hard abrader would provide more visible scratches, not a polish.

The activity most responsible for the attrition pattern is contact with the rattan pot carrier and with the human hand. On some pots there is about a 1-cm region near the lip that does not come in contact with the rattan carrier and is not polished. The hand also contacts a similar area of the pot while it is carried hot or cold. The most typical way to carry an empty pot is with one hand; four fingers inside the pot and the thumb

Figure 6.13. Polished surface on the upper exterior side consists of fine linear scratches (length of frame is approximately 4.5 mm).

running along the neck of the vessel and contacting the same region as the rattan carrier.

There are also some random fine scratches similar to those found on the entire vessel exterior. These are not as deeply entrenched as scratches on portions of the lower vessel, and they also tend to align with the rim as one moves up near the neck. The fine scratches are caused by small abraders that are harder than the pottery surface (remembering that the pottery surface consists of resin and carbon).

The activity responsible for these scratches is scrubbing by hand as the pot is washed with water, sand, charcoal, leaves, rice chaff, or a wet rag. The scratches are not as prevalent here as on lower parts of the vessel because the soot layer is much thinner. Recall that the primary reason to scrub the exterior of the vessels is to remove some of the soot. The scratches tend to align horizontally near the top of the vessel because it is difficult to scrub vertically in this region.

As on the lower portions of the vessel, scrubbing with the leaves, or rice chaff, or some other soft material, is one activity that does not leave a trace. In this case it may contribute to the polish, but that is difficult to determine.

Although this area has some very informative use traces, it is likely that they would not survive in the depositional environment. The carbon layer may survive, but the resin layer is likely to decompose in most environments. What would be left is a ceramic surface that is clear of most abrasive traces.

5. *Rim* (Figure 6.1). This area is restricted to just the vessel lip, and it is the smallest attritional region discussed. Two use-attrition traces are found on the rim. The first is linear scratches, oriented horizontally, that eventually remove the exterior surface of the rim. The second is chips that can range in size from 1 millimeter to several centimeters.

Several activities are most responsible for the use-attrition traces of the rim. These include (1) contact with the ground as the vessel exteriors are washed; (2) covering and uncovering the pots with metal lids; (3) contact with metal or wood utensils during stirring and serving; (4) stacking of the pots for transport or storage; (5) grasping the pots by hand; and (6) scrubbing the pots with sand, charcoal, leaves, rice chaff, a wet rag, or any combination thereof.

All cooking vessels have linear scratches on the rim that travel in a direction parallel to the rim edge. As a vessel is used more frequently, the rim surface becomes completely removed, and in many cases the rim has been worn flat (Figure 6.14). Some pots are in the intermediate stage; areas of the rim are completely removed whereas others are scratched, but the surfaces are intact.

The scratches on the rim suggest that there is a directional contact with an abrader that consists of small particles that are harder than the ceramic. Pitting is also frequent and is more common than pedestalled temper in this region. This suggests that the directional contact is forceful but that the abrader consists of material that has a diameter smaller than the distance between temper particles.

The activity responsible for this abrasive patch is contact with the ground during exterior washing. As the exterior of the pot is washed, both the midexterior side and the rim contact the ground as the pot is rotated.

The attrition on the rim caused by washing is the only exterior attrition that varies slightly between the vegetable/meat and rice cooking pots. Although it is difficult to quantify, the vegetable/meat cooking pots almost always have more abrasion on the rim than the rice cooking pots. This is because of the shape of the pot rather than more intensive washing. The vegetable/meat pots have a wider mouth and a more

Figure 6.14. Rim worn flat because of contact with the ground during washing.

outflared rim and thus present a more vulnerable surface than the rice cooking vessels; during washing, more force is placed upon the rims of the vegetable/meat pots.

The second attritional trace on the rims is chips (Figure 6.15). About 70% of all daily-use cooking vessels in the village of Guina-ang have chipped rims. They vary widely in size and shape, but most appear to have been formed by single impacts. The shape of the chip can sometimes provide information about the angle and direction of the blow; often a point of impact can be discerned. In most cases the impact comes from the top of the rim, but side blows are also common. Less can be said about the abrader that causes the chipping than most other forms of surface attrition. Certainly a blow from a material harder than the ceramic can cause chipping but, if the impact is of great enough force, an object softer than the ceramic can also cause a chip.

Many use activities can chip the rim. Pots are covered with metal lids, and occasionally the lids are dropped on the rim, causing a chip. During a single cooking episode, the vegetable/meat cooking pots are covered and recovered many more times than the rice pots because the boiling of vegetables or meat requires closer monitoring. If many of the rim chips are acquired as a result of covering, one would expect the

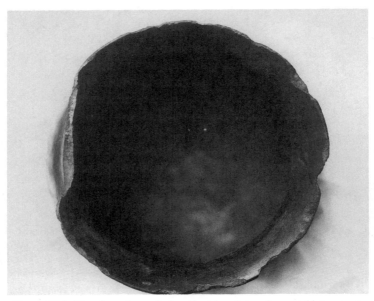

Figure 6.15. View from above of a heavily chipped rim of a vegetable/meat pot.

vegetable/meat cooking pots to have more rim chips than the rice cooking vessels. But this is not the case. Out of the 220 daily-use rice cooking
pots in the village of Guina-ang, 70% had one or more chips on the rim.
A total of 313 vegetable/meat cooking pots were in daily use during our
field season, and 70% of those were also chipped. The process of covering the vessel does not seem to be responsible for the chips in the rim.

The rims of cooking vessels are most often chipped while the pots
are carried or moved within the house or transported to the washing
spots. Impacts to the rim were most often observed while the pots were
being picked up; contact was made with other pots or with shelves or
items in the house. Contact on the rims of pots also occurred as they
were being carried to and from the wash spot. Often, at least two pots
were carried by hand or stacked with other items in a wash basin.

Contact between a metal or wood utensil and the rim during stirring or serving can also cause chips. After the contents of the vegeta-
ble/meat pots are stirred, the ladle is often tapped on the rim. But
because vegetable/meat cooking pots do not have more rim chips than
rice pots, the contact between ladle and rim is also thought to be a
minor cause of chipping.

The chips can also provide information about the direction of motion as the pots are rotated during washing. Directional movement can be determined by the same principle as was done with the attrition on the lower and midexterior sides. A fresh chip has sharp edges that are vulnerable to abrasion. This is especially true of the edge that faces the abrasive action. Both edges will abrade, but one edge of the chip (seen on the left of Figure 6.16) will abrade at a much higher rate.

As with all the exterior parts of the vessel, a number of activities contact the rim but do not leave a trace. One consistent activity that would seemingly leave an abrasive trace is covering with metal lids. Vegetable/meat cooking pots may be uncovered and covered as many as 10 times during one cooking episode, whereas rice cooking pots will be uncovered just a few times. Because there appears to be no difference in the amount of chipping and there is no other form of abrasion that can be linked to covering, this activity is one that does not leave a trace.

The linear scratches caused by contact with the ground during washing are such a dominant trace that they overwhelm subtle traces, such as those formed by contact with hands as the pots are carried and manipulated, scrubbing with charcoal or leaves, and contact with the cooking utensils during stirring and serving.

This concludes the discussion of the attritional traces on the exterior of Kalinga cooking vessels. The vegetable/meat and rice cooking pots have markedly similar exterior attritional traces. Although there are some subtle differences in activities that contact the exterior of these two types of cooking vessels, none of them was recorded in the attritional traces. The dominant attritional activity for the exterior of cooking pots was washing. The vegetable/meat and rice cooking pots are washed in similar ways, and the resultant traces often obliterate more subtle traces that result from less abrasive activities. The important point is that all Kalinga

Figure 6.16. A rim chip with the left side of the chip more abraded than the right. Pot is rotated clockwise while washing, and the left side of the chip is more susceptible to abrasion.

cooking pots share a common activity; all pots are placed over a fire to heat their contents. This common activity, cooking, gets the pots dirty. The shared washing activity among cooking vessels is reflected in nearly identical exterior use-attrition patterns.

Four attritional patches on the interior of Kalinga cooking vessels are discussed next. In contrast to the pot exteriors, attrition on vessel interiors reflects what was cooked. Consequently, vegetable/meat and rice cooking pots can be distinguished based upon attrition in all four regions.

6. *Interior rim and neck* (Figure 6.1). All interior surfaces, including the rim and neck, have a coat of resin. The interior rim and neck are discussed in the same section because together they provide the entryway to a cooking vessel. Two types of surface attrition are found in this region. The first is abrasion, usually resulting in exposed and slightly pedestalled temper on the interior neck, and the second is thermal spalling on the interior rim.

Activities that have the potential to cause an attritional trace on the interior rim and neck include (1) covering and uncovering the vessel with a metal lid; (2) stirring the contents of the vessel and serving the food with either wood or metal utensils; (3) carrying the vessels; (4) placement of the pots next to the fire; and (5) washing with charcoal, sand, leaves, and rice chaff.

On vessels that have evidence of being used many times (i.e., the pot is completely sooted and the vessel has abrasive patches), there will be abrasion on the interior neck, especially at the narrowest point of the vessel opening. On vessels with this abrasion, temper is exposed and often pedestalled slightly (Figure 6.17). Usually this abrasion is not easily seen with the naked eye, but by touch the slightly roughened surface caused by the pedestalled temper is apparent. This pattern suggests a relatively gentle abrasion and that the abrader has surfaces that can expose but not totally pedestal the temper. This contrasts with other portions of the vessel, such as the base, in which the temper particles become abraded to a point of exposing nearly of all their surface. The abrader in this case consists of surfaces larger then the distance between temper particles and the abrader is harder than the ceramic material.

Abrasion on the neck occurs on both vegetable/meat and rice cooking pots if they have been used a number of times, but the former has heavier neck abrasion. Because the rice cooking pots have a more constricted orifice than the vegetable/meat cooking vessels, one could infer

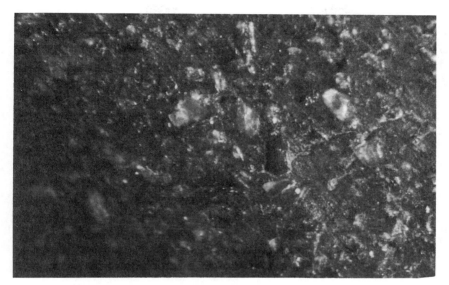

Figure 6.17. Temper exposed by abrasion on the interior neck.

from both vessel morphology and abrasion traces that there is differential access to the contents of the vessel. This illustrates a concurrence of both intended and actual use.

The activities most responsible for the abrasion on the interior neck are stirring and serving with wood and metal utensils. In the case of the vegetable/meat cooking pots, contact between the interior neck and a metal or wood ladle (*pa-oc*) is made numerous times during one cooking episode (Figure 6.18). The vessels are stirred a number of times, water is often added, and the vegetables or meat are checked often to determine when they have finished cooking. The primary contact between the utensils and the interior neck of the rice cooking pots occurs as the rice is served (Figure 6.19). Only once during the cooking episode is a utensil placed into the pot. Thus the differential abrasion on the neck of vegetable/meat and rice cooking pots is a factor of the number of times the contents are manipulated with utensils. Another factor is that in 83% of the households, both metal and wood ladles are used for stirring the vegetables or meat. In contrast, 71% of the households used wood spatulas (*edgus*) for serving the rice. The metal ladles, in this case aluminum, are harder than the wood (coconut shell) ladles and should cause more material loss in an abrasive situation. Therefore, two factors are

Figure 6.18. Contact is made between the metal ladle and the interior of the pot as the vegetables are served.

responsible for the greater abrasion on the interior neck of the vegetable/meat cooking pot. First, there are many more contact situations during vegetable and meat cooking, and second, metal rather than wood utensils are used more frequently in vegetable/meat pots.

The second form of attrition on the interior rim and neck are thermal spalls. They are most frequently found on the midinterior side, but they also occur on the interior rim. Thermal spalls are roughly circular in shape and range in diameter from 1 to 3 mm (Figure 6.20). They are caused as water vaporizes in the body of the ceramic and the escaping steam spalls off a small portion of the interior surface. Four conditions are necessary for thermal spalling: (1) moisture in the vessel wall; (2) heat; (3) the interior surface must have a permeability lower than the interior of the vessel wall; and (4) immediately next to the low-permeability surface, there must be less moisture than in the vessel wall interior.

Thermal spalls are almost exclusively found on rice cooking pots. They are formed during the third stage of rice cooking as the pots are placed next to the fire in the simmer position (Figure 6.21). At this point

Figure 6.19. As rice is served, contact is made between the wood utensil and the interior neck of the vessel.

in rice cooking, the remaining water in the vessels is absorbed into the rice. The pots are rotated several times while in this position to prevent burning. In some cases pots are left in this position too long, and all free water in the vessel is removed. This is the point at which thermal spalls are formed. The free water in the pots disappears, and water in the vessel wall begins to vaporize. It escapes in a direction away from the heat source toward the interior of the vessel. A thermal spall is produced because the water vapor must pass through the interior surface that has lower permeability (recall that the interior is smoothed and also coated with resin). A spall is not formed in every cooking episode, only when the rice is left in the simmer position too long. The rice next to the vessel wall in this case will be dry and slightly burned.

Vegetable/meat cooking pots are occasionally put into the simmer position to keep the contents warm, but thermal spalls are not formed. That is because the pot is at least half-filled with water, and the vessel wall stays saturated. One prerequisite of thermal spalling, having a dry surface opposite the surface with applied heat, is not met. Moreover, thermal spalls are never found on the interior base on any of

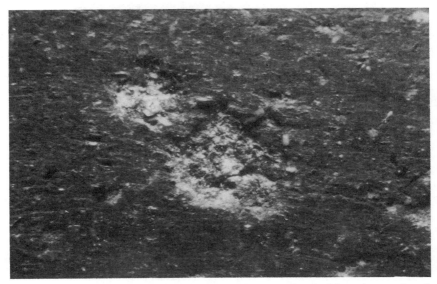

Figure 6.20. Thermal spalls on the interior of rice cooking pots (length of frame is approximately 7 mm).

the cooking vessels because, while the pots are on the fire, they always contain some water.

In summary, there are two primary forms of attrition on the interior rim and neck, and both provide information about pottery use activity. From the abrasion on the neck one can infer that the contents of vegetable/meat cooking pots are manipulated more than those of rice cooking vessels. Moreover, thermal spalls, found only on rice cooking pots, suggest that vessels are placed next to a heat source while the vessel wall is saturated but moisture inside the vessel has been removed.

But there are a number of use activities that do not leave a trace on the interior rim and neck region. The most striking activity not represented is covering of the pots with metal lids. No evidence of this is found on the cooking pots. Moreover, vegetable/meat pots are covered and uncovered many more times in one cooking episode than the rice cooking vessels, but there is no trace of this. There is also no evidence of carrying the vessels. When the pot is empty, it is often carried by one hand with the thumb resting along the exterior neck and the four fingers grasping the interior rim and neck. No attritional traces can be linked directly to the hand contact. Washing contact also does not leave a trace.

Figure 6.21. The rice cooking pot sits next to the fire in the simmer position while the vegetable/meat pot is on the fire.

Because very little food residue is found on the interior rim and neck of pots after cooking, scrubbing the interior involves more rinsing out with water than hard scrubbing.

7. *Upper interior side* (Figure 6.1). Two attritional traces are found in this region: pits and thermal spalls. The thermal spalls, found only on the rice cooking pots, occur less frequently here than on the interior rim and especially the midinterior side. The pits occur only on the vegetable/meat cooking pots, and they are found as isolated marks, often angled up toward the rim.

Several activities have the potential to cause an attritional trace and they include (1) stirring of the vegetable/meat cooking pot with metal or wood ladles; (2) placement of the rice cooking pot next to the fire; and (3) scrubbing the surface with sand, charcoal, leaves, a wet cloth, or rice chaff.

The vegetable/meat cooking pots often have pits or nicks on the upper interior side. The pits have the appearance of single impact marks (Figure 6.22). The shape and orientation of the marks provide information about the direction of the blow and type of abrader. The pits are angled toward the rim, and the point of initiation for each mark is found

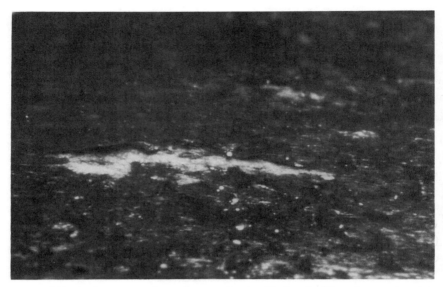

Figure 6.22. Single impact marks on the upper interior side (length of frame is approximately 7 mm).

usually on the lower side. The attributes of these marks suggest that the abrader was harder than the ceramic; it was traveling at a relatively high velocity, and it was moving in a clockwise and slightly upward direction within the vessel.

The activity responsible for this mark is the stirring and serving of vegetables or meat. If an individual uses his or her right hand, the ladle is moved in a clockwise direction. The ladle ends up at a position nearest to the stirrer with an upward motion that often impacts the upper interior side. That the majority of households now use metal ladles, instead of the traditional type made of coconut shell, may be responsible for more of these impact marks, but the sample of pots from households that only employed the latter was too small for comparison. It is possible, however, that a coconut shell ladle could also cause such a mark if the velocity at impact was great. It is interesting to note that the smaller vegetable/meat cooking pots have far fewer marks of this type. This is not because of a different use activity but rather a result of the smaller internal area of the vessel; it appears that the ladle does not generate enough velocity at impact with the upper interior side to cause the types of marks found on the larger vegetable/meat cooking pots.

The second major type of attrition is thermal spalls, which are found only on the rice cooking pots. There are far fewer spalls here than on the midinterior side (discussed later) but they are all formed by the same process. The pots are exposed to a heat source while there is water in the vessel wall but no longer any moisture on the vessel surface opposite the heat source. There are fewer spalls on the upper interior side than on the midinterior side because the former is farther from the heat source and it has an angled surface that serves to deflect some of the heat.

On the upper interior side, as on the remainder of the cooking vessel interiors, there are fine scratches that travel in random directions, although there is a preference for the scratches to travel parallel to the rim. From the attributes of these marks one can infer that (1) they were produced by a fine abrader and a relatively gentle abrasive action; (2) there was movement involved in the interaction between abrader and ceramic; and (3) the movement traveled in a random direction.

The activity responsible is the washing of the interiors of the vessels with sand, charcoal, leaves, rice chaff, and sometimes a cloth rag, or any combination thereof. While placing the pot on the ground at an angle and rotating the vessel in a clockwise direction, the interiors are scrubbed. Because boiling does not leave much food residue and rice cooking is done with leaves coating the interior of the pot, little internal washing is necessary.

All major use activities that affect the upper interior side leave traces. Moreover, the vegetable/meat and rice cooking pots have unique attritional traces that reflect different kinds of cooking.

8. *Midinterior side* (Figure 6.1). Besides the fine scratches found on the interior of all cooking vessels, only one other attritional trace is found in this region, thermal spalls, and only on the rice cooking pots. The two activities that could potentially cause attrition are (1) placement of the rice cooking pots next to the fire during the third stage of cooking; and (2) washing the vessels with sand, charcoal, leaves, rice chaff, cloth rags, or any combination thereof.

Thermal spalls are found from this region up to the rim, but the greatest number of these marks are found on the midinterior side. Individual spalls are usually about 2 mm in diameter and are never very deep (Figure 6.20). The greatest concentration of spalls coincides with the internal patch of carbonization on the rice cooking pots (discussed in Chapter 7). On some vessels the spalls are so numerous that the entire surface is removed. A thermal spall can be distinguished from other attritional traces in several ways. A pit caused by the thermal spall is usually round or nearly round, and a cross-section of a pit would either be hemispherical or conical. The edge of the pit forms a sharp break, and there is no evidence of impact or abrasion. In many of the pits created by the thermal spall there is also microscopic cracking (Figure 6.23) probably caused by the escaping steam.

The process of thermal spall formation can be understood by noting the lack of thermal spalls on vegetable/meat cooking pots. The latter are sometimes put into the simmer position next to the fire exactly like the rice cooking pots. This is done while cooking the specialty sticky rice (*chaycot*) or simply to keep the food hot after it is taken off the fire. Probably because cooking sticky rice entails stirring and other manipulation during heating, vegetable/meat cooking pots with their bigger orifices are desired. Although any one vegetable/meat pot will not spend as much time in the simmer position as a similar rice cooking vessel, it is significant that no thermal spalls were observed on the vegetable/meat pots. That is because in all cases when vegetable/meat pots are in the simmer position there is water on the interior surface of the pots; when

Figure 6.23. Microscopic cracking on the interior of a thermal spall (length of frame is approximately 3 mm).

cooking vegetables or meat the pots are half-filled with water, and the water from the sticky rice is not removed to the same degree as is done for the standard rice cooking. The one requirement for thermal spall formation, no water on the low-permeability interior surface, is never met in the vegetable/meat pots.

Fine scratches are the same on the midinterior side as they are on the rest of the interior so they are not discussed further.

9. *Lower interior side and base* (Figure 6.1). These two regions are discussed together because they share attritional traces. Thermal spalling may extend into this area, but the primary traces are the fine scratches, caused by washing, and the removal of the surface of some of the heavily used vegetable/meat cooking pots. Attritional activities that affect the lower interior side and base include (1) scrubbing by hand with sand, leaves, charcoal, rice chaff, a rag, or any combination thereof; and (2) stirring and serving the contents of the vessels with wood and metal utensils.

The fine scratches from washing are similar to those on the rest of the cooking pot interiors and are not discussed further. The only other abrasive trace occurs on the vegetable/meat cooking pots. Rice cooking pots have no attrition on the lower interior side and base because (1) the interiors are often covered with a layer of leaves, and (2) the wooden spatula (*edgus*) used to serve the rice rarely makes any contact with this region of the pot. There is, however, evidence for slight abrasion on the vegetable/meat cooking vessels. Abrasion in this area consists merely of removing the interior coat of resin and then abrading away some of the ceramic surface to expose but not pedestal the temper particles. But even in the heavily used vessels, abrasion on the lower interior side and base is never great. This suggests that this region had contact with a gentle abrader with a surface that is larger than the distance between temper particles. The activity responsible for this abrasion is the stirring of the contents of vegetable/meat cooking pots with a wood or metal ladle.

DISCUSSION AND SUMMARY

Table 6.1 summarizes a comparison of use attrition on the vegetable/meat and rice cooking pots. One can conclude from this comparison that activities that affect the exterior of vessels are the same for all cooking pots, with only some exceptions. All cooking pots get dirty and are

Table 6.1. Use Attrition of Vegetable/Meat and Rice Cooking Pots

	Vegetable/meat pots	Rice pots
Exterior base	Circular abrasive patch with pits, scratches, and pedestalled temper	Same
Lower exterior side	Fine, randomly oriented scratches and deep, linear scratches parallel to the rim	Same
Midexterior side	Fine, randomly oriented scratches and deep, linear scratches parallel to the rim	Same
Upper exterior side	Polish	Same
Rim	Deep, linear scratches and chips	Same with less linear scratching
Interior rim and neck	Moderate abrasion with slightly pedestalled temper	Thermal spalls and no abrasion
Upper interior side	Pits	Thermal spalls
Midinterior side	Fine scratches	Thermal spalls, fine scratches
Lower interior side and base	Fine scratches and slightly exposed temper	Thermal spalls, fine scratches

washed in a similar fashion; washing traces dominate the exterior of cooking pots. One important finding is that I was able to determine the directionality of the abrasive traces caused by washing. Certainly it is not that significant that I can tell the direction that women rotate their pots during washing (though it could be a method to determine handedness); the importance of this finding is that it defined criteria for determining the directionality of an abrasive trace.

The most striking finding of this analysis is that the pots used to cook different items had very different interior attritional traces. From these traces one can infer a number of use activities. For example, there is little evidence of stirring or other forms of manipulation in the rice cooking pots, but the vegetable/meat cooking vessels have numerous marks that suggest that the contents were stirred during use. The angle of contact and direction of the stirring motion can also be inferred from these traces. In addition, thermal spalls on the midinterior side of the rice cooking pots suggest that they were placed next to a heat source while the vessel walls were still saturated, but the liquid inside the pots had been removed.

This study has demonstrated that by applying a few general principles regarding the interaction between ceramic and abrader or attritional source, one can infer specific patterned activities of pottery use. Kalinga pots are not unique in being "ripe" with use-attrition information. All low-fired ceramic vessels subject to repeated action in use will acquire traces that can be linked to particular use activities.

There are certainly general and specific types of information that can be obtained about pottery use from use attrition. Study of attrition can and should be an integral part of analyses designed to investigate pottery use. Further implications of this analysis are discussed in the concluding chapter.

Chapter **7**

Use Alteration:
Carbon Deposition

Building on the work of Hally (1983a), this chapter discusses the processes that govern carbon deposition on pottery. This includes a discussion of the carbon patterns on Kalinga cooking vessels and an exploration of the factors that are important in this process. Several experiments are performed to determine how factors such as distance to fire, type of wood, and the presence of moisture affect carbon deposition.

Carbon on the surface of pottery results from combustion of organic material and deposition of the resultant carbonized matter on or in some cases into the porous and permeable ceramic wall. A number of activities can deposit carbon on or in a pottery surface, such as firing pottery in an environment with reduced oxygen, cooking over an open fire, and even burning of a structure. The carbon deposition of concern here takes place during use of a vessel over an open fire. Both interior and exterior carbon deposits are considered.

Exterior carbon deposits, referred to here as soot, have been used to infer vessel function (see Hally 1983a and Chapter 2). Soot deposits have been employed most often to determine whether vessels were used for cooking over an open fire (e.g., Hill 1970:49; Turner and Lofgren 1966:123), but soot deposits and carbon deposits on the surface of pottery in general can provide additional information about vessel use. Exterior and interior carbon deposits inform us on how the pot was positioned over a fire, what was cooked, and some of the activities involved in cooking.

In the most involved analysis to date of sooting patterns and related

147

patches of oxidation, Hally (1983a; see also Henrickson 1990) offers several inferences about the use of vessels excavated from two Barnett phase sites in northwestern Georgia. He identified 12 morphological vessel types in the ceramic assemblage and found that some pots were used over an open fire and others were not. Hally determined that two vessel types, identical except in size, were used differently; the smaller type was used over a fire, but the larger one was not. Moreover, two vessel types similar in size and shape but different in composition were both used over a fire but in different ways. One of the vessels did not have an oxidized patch on the base, which suggested to Hally that it was suspended over the fire rather than being set on pot supports near the flame. Hally (1983a), however, looked only at exterior soot deposits. Interior carbon deposits are formed by different, albeit related, processes and provide more information about cooking-related activities.

CARBON DEPOSITS ON KALINGA VESSELS

Because there are basically two forms of cooking in Kalinga, pottery collected from the Guina-ang households provides an informative case study; vegetable/meat and rice cooking have many similar but also some different cooking-related activities. It is found that all Kalinga cooking pots share many traits of interior and exterior carbon deposits but that there are some patterns unique to either the vegetable/meat or rice cooking vessels.

Interior Carbon Deposits

Carbon deposition on vessel interiors is caused, simply, by charring of food. Food residues that adhere to or are absorbed into a vessel surface become carbonized when the pot is heated to a sufficient temperature. Interior carbon deposits, unlike exterior carbon deposits, penetrate the body of the vessel. Carbon deposition on pottery interiors is governed primarily by three factors: heat intensity, moisture in the vessel interior, and source of heat. On Kalinga cooking pots, interior carbon deposits become part of the vessel wall and cannot be removed during washing (although burned remnants of food that adhere to the surface will be removed).

Kobayashi (n.d.) divides the Kalinga pattern of pottery carbon deposition into four classes: (1) no carbon deposits, (2) a patch of carbon on the midinterior side, (3) a patch of carbon on the midinterior side and interior base, and (4) a continuous patch of carbon from the upper interior side to the base. Although he found that these classes represent progressive stages in interior carbon deposition (i.e., as the pots are used they progress from Stage 1 through Stage 4), by far the most frequent pattern is Stage 3, a patch of carbon on the midinterior side and on the interior base (see Figures 7.1 and 7.2). Most daily-use cooking pots reach stage three and remain there throughout their use lives. The surprising finding is that the interior carbon patterns on both vegetable/meat and rice cooking pots have some similar features despite very different cooking activities associated with each vessel type. But this is a clear case of equifinality; different processes are responsible for carbon deposition in the interiors of the two vessel types.

Rice Cooking Pots

The carbon patches on the interior of rice cooking pots are formed during two stages of cooking. The patch on the base is formed, in part, during

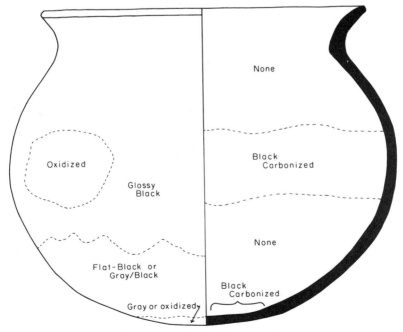

Figure 7.1. Carbon deposits on rice pots.

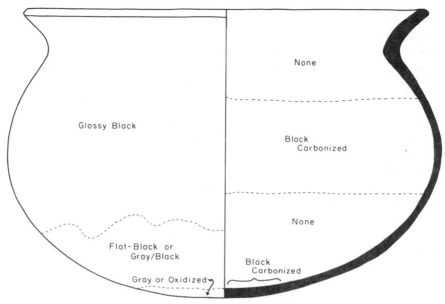

Figure 7.2. Carbon deposits on vegetable/meat pot.

the first stage of rice cooking as the contents are brought to a boil (see Figure 4.2). As the rice is heated and water is removed, a residue the consistency of paste collects on the interior surface. The hottest area of the pot during this stage of cooking is the base; if enough water is removed at this point of rice cooking, the pastelike residue carbonizes. It is likely, however, that most of the basal carbonization occurs as the pot sits—on a bed of coals—in the simmer position during the third stage of rice cooking (Figure 4.14). The heat from the coals, in association with the reduced moisture of the rice, is thought to produce the majority of the basal carbonization.

The carbon patch on the midinterior side is also formed as the vessel is placed to the side of the fire in the simmer position (Figure 4.14). If the pot is left too long in the simmer position, moisture in the vessel is removed, and the rice becomes visibly charred in the area nearest the fire. When this occurs, a round patch of carbon will form, and thermal spalls (see Chapter 6) can be produced. Because the pots are rotated at least three times while in this stage of cooking, several patches of carbon can be produced. Although carbon is not formed during every cooking episode (charring of the rice is not desired), after many uses the individual carbon patches will grow into a continuous ring of carbon on the mid-interior side.

Vegetable/Meat Cooking Pots

The vegetable/meat cooking pots have the same general pattern of carbon deposits as rice cooking pots (Figures 7.1 and 7.2), but for very different reasons. Although Kobayashi (n.d.) found that vegetable/meat pots are less likely than rice cooking pots to have the patch of carbon on the base, the most frequent pattern is to have a carbon deposit on the base and on the midinterior side.

With the exception of cooking a sweet, sticky rice, food in the vegetable/meat pots is boiled. Water is put into the vessel up to about the level of the midinterior side, and the vegetable or meat is boiled. The pots are left to boil until the contents are cooked, and water is added when needed. The ring of carbon on the midinterior side is created by particles of food that adhere to the vessel wall at and slightly above the water line. The particles burn and produce patches of carbon. Eventually the entire midinterior side is covered by a carbon patch. This patch on the vegetable/meat pots is often slightly wider and may extend higher up the vessel wall than a similar carbon patch on the midinterior side of rice pots (see Figures 7.1 and 7.2).

The patch of carbon on the interior base of the vegetable/meat pots forms at the point exposed to the greatest heat. The interior coating of resin on cooking pots reduces water permeability but does not stop it. During cooking, water rich in organic matter penetrates the pottery wall and is not removed by washing. It is thought that these minute organic particles become carbonized during the next cooking episode. In the earliest stage of cooking, before water has permeated into the body, the temperature of the exterior base is the hottest. At this point, it is believed that the organic matter, deposited in previous cooking episodes, carbonizes.

This patch of carbon may form less frequently in the vegetable/meat cooking pots than in the rice cooking pots because the the wall of former vessel type is saturated with water throughout all but a few minutes in the earliest stage of cooking. Moreover, the cooking of some foods, like many vegetables, produces little food residue. In contrast, cooking of sticky rice (*chaycot*) in vegetable/meat pots should consistently produce a patch of carbon on the interior base. Some varieties of *chaycot,* cooked only on special occasions, become very thick and require constant stirring to avoid burning. It is anticipated that a carbon deposit is almost always formed on the base of vegetable/meat pots when they are used for cooking the thick form of *chaycot.*

All three factors important in interior carbon deposition (i.e., heat intensity, source of heat, and moisture) are illustrated in Kalinga cooking pots. In both rice and vegetable/meat cooking pots, the heat of greatest intensity is focused on the base. It is common for cooking pots to have a patch of carbon on the interior base. In both the rice and vegetable/meat pots, food residue carbonizes at the point of greatest heat when moisture is removed from the vessel wall. Moisture, heat sources, and intensity also play a role in the deposition of carbon on the midinterior side of rice cooking pots. While the rice pots are set next to the fire in the simmer position, the focused heat will create a patch of carbon as the rice becomes charred. The rice burns slightly at this point because the moisture in the rice pot has been removed.

The interior carbon deposits, therefore, reflect the cooking activity. It is true that the vegetable/meat and rice cooking pots have a somewhat similar pattern of interior carbon deposition but, with a large sample of pots and especially with the pattern of exterior soot, one could infer that the carbon patterns were created by different activities.

Exterior Carbon Deposits

The exterior carbon, or soot, on Kalinga vessels is caused by the deposition of the by-products of wood combustion. Soot is defined as "a family of particulate materials consisting of variable quantities of carbonaceous and inorganic solids in conjunction with adsorbed and occluded organic tars and resins" (Medalia and Rivin 1982:481). Wood combustion creates volatile pyrolysis products, which include hydrocarbons and carbon monoxide, and a carbonaceous residue. Soot can be produced at two points in this process: as a direct product of the carbonaceous residue, and if the oxygen level is low the hydrocarbons will crack and produce soot (Evans *et al.* 1981:1985).

The literature on fuel combustion by-products is voluminous; the primary sources are produced by those who are working on controlling airborne emissions from fuel combustion and from research on carbon black, a combustion product that is exploited commercially (see Goldberg 1985). But there has been little research on the forms of soot produced by low temperature and uncontrolled wood combustion

(Medalia and Rivin 1982:484), and there has been, to my knowledge, no analysis of the soot produced by wood and deposited on pottery. Soot produced by an open-air fire and deposited on a ceramic pot, often kept cool by its contents, is a situation that is not encountered by researchers other than archaeologists. Moreover, what is of interest is soot that remains after a pot is washed, a situation not addressed by researchers in other fields. Consequently, the description of Kalinga pottery sooting and the experiments that follow rely heavily on basic visual description. Though the various soot types found on pottery likely will have distinctive chemical and physical properties, it is beyond the scope of the present study to analyze their compositions. This study relies heavily on describing visually the sooting patterns and then understanding the processes, by experiment, that govern soot deposition on cooking pots.

Hally (1983a) was one of the first to attempt to understand the process of soot deposition on pottery. His experiments identified two kinds of soot. The first is a dull black layer directly above the fire that probably consists of solid carbon. This layer could be largely removed when rubbed. The second deposit had a lustrous quality and was found on the sides and rim. This layer could not be removed by rubbing; Hally (1983a:8) suggests that this soot deposit consists of oxidized resins and solid carbon. He further suggests that distance from the flame is the important variable in the formation of the two types of soot.

The Barnett phase ceramics analyzed by Hally (1983a) followed a similar pattern. Soot was thickest on the midexterior sides, and it became thinner near the rim and base—some even had oxidized patches on the base. This suggested to Hally (1983a) that the pots were set directly over or in the fire and in some cases suspended, at a slightly greater height, over the fire.

Sooting on Kalinga pots also conforms to the pattern described by Hally (1983a). (When I refer to the sooting pattern, it also includes areas that are oxidized or have no soot.) The most typical pattern, illustrated in Figures 7.1 and 7.2, consists of two distinct patches of soot. The first extends from the base to the lower exterior side (although the location of the transition between patches varies with pot size). The patch consists of a thin layer of dull black or sometimes gray soot. The entire base of many pots is also unsooted, and the original ceramic surface is exposed.

At the lower exterior side there is a transition between this patch and a patch of soot that extends to the rim (Figures 7.1 and 7.2).

The soot in this region has a glossy or lustrous quality (see Figure 6.2). In heavily used pots, the soot will build up, in an area from the lower exterior side to the upper exterior side and eventually begin to chip and exfoliate. The glossy soot scratches easily and this entire region, which comes in contact with the ground during washing, has numerous scratches. Washing also contributes to the chipping away of the soot as it builds up. The soot in this region is thickest at the midsection and thinner toward the base and rim.

A third type of soot is deposited on Kalinga vessels during cooking. This layer is dull, gray, and ashy and usually covers the entire vessel, except in the area protected by the pot rests, during every cooking episode. All of this soot is removed during washing. The soot that remains cannot be removed by washing and seems permanently affixed; Kalinga sherds excavated from a midden in Puapo (a nearby settlement) are still covered with exterior soot. The soot that cannot be removed by washing is the focus of this analysis.

The pattern just described and illustrated in Figures 7.1 and 7.2 forms the core of Kalinga pottery sooting. There are some differences between vegetable/meat and rice cooking pots, described later, but all Kalinga cooking vessels (except the roasting pots) have this basic sooting pattern. Based on what is known about pottery sooting (see Hally 1983a), several statements can be made about Kalinga cooking. First, the pots are set above the source of heat, as opposed to being directly placed in the fire. (There is no exterior soot evidence for the placement of rice pots on the bed of coals while in the simmer position. Rice cooking pots do not have significantly larger oxidized patches on the base than do vegetable/meat pots. In most cases, the "bed of coals" underlying rice pots consists only of a few burning fragments. Heat generated from the coals does not seem to be hot enough to oxidize the basal soot.) Moreover, on some vessels, especially if they have not been used many times, there is evidence of the hearth pot supports. In any one cooking episode, sooting does not occur directly above the points of contact between the pot and the three pot supports (Figure 7.3). This provides additional evidence that the pots were supported above the fire, in this case by three pot supports.

Second, it appears that distance above the heat source is an important factor in the Kalinga sooting pattern. As one moves from the base of the pot to the rim there are two and sometimes three patches of soot. This same pattern is noted by Hally (1983a), and it confirms his notion

Figure 7.3. Pottery sooting pattern. Note that the soot does not appear directly over the pot support.

that soot is deposited in distinct patches based upon distance away from the heat source.

Finally, the core Kalinga pottery sooting pattern illustrates that both the rice and vegetable/meat cooking pots take part in similar cooking activities. With few exceptions, both types of cooking pots have the same basic sooting pattern. But one feature of exterior sooting does distinguish vegetable/meat from the rice cooking pots.

Rice cooking pots often have an oxidized patch on the midexterior side (Figure 7.1) formed while the pot sits next to the fire in the simmer position. The patches correspond to the carbonized patches on the interior and also the interior thermal spalls. The oxidized patches on the exterior are not formed during every cooking episode. For the soot to oxidize, the pot must stay in the same position for a relatively long time, especially if the soot is thick. Moreover, the oxidized patches, if they exist, will be resooted during the next cooking episode. So, for the patches to be identified, they must have formed the last time rice was cooked. This contrasts with the carbonized patches on the interior of the vessel; they probably form each time an oxidized patch forms on the exterior, but they are also permanent, eventually forming a continual band on the midinterior side of rice cooking pots. In fact, most oxidized patches on the exterior of vessels are associated with a carbonized patch on the interior. The opposite, however, is not true. Because oxidized patches on both the exterior base and on the midexterior side can be resooted in the next cooking episode, they are not always positively correlated with interior patches of carbonization.

Oxidized patches also appear on the exterior base of Kalinga pottery in a situation in which they do not become resooted. When a pot becomes worn out, *na-u-log*, it is no longer used for cooking. Pots that are *na-u-log* do not have an interior coating of resin, and the contents of the pots, according to the people, are difficult—if not impossible—to bring to a boil. It is believed that the interior resin has worn away, permitting moisture to get into the vessel wall and interfere with the heating process. Experiments have shown (cf. Schiffer 1990) that pots without an impermeable surface treatment have a much lower heating effectiveness and may be unable to boil water.

The interesting feature of *na-u-log* pots is that they frequently have an oxidized patch on the exterior base, and the overall sooting pattern changes slightly. The oxidized patches are often larger than those on pots that are not *na-u-log,* and in some cases the thin gray layer of soot is absent; thus there is a transition directly from the oxidized patch to the glossy soot layer. Oxidized patches on cooking vessels can be formed by high heat intensity or the application of heat in the absence of soot. This situation could occur if a pot was set very near a fire or if the fuel was very clean burning. However, in the case of *na-u-log* pots, neither the fuel nor the position on the hearth is any different. The only feature of the cooking process that may be different for *na-u-log* pots is that they would be on the hearth longer than pots with the resin still intact. But it appears that moisture in the vessel wall may play a role in soot deposition and the associated discoloration caused by oxidation. Experiments described later investigate this possibility and also clarify the general process of soot formation.

EXPERIMENTS ON EXTERIOR SOOT FORMATION

Although sooting of Kalinga pottery appears to follow a typical sooting pattern seen on other pottery assemblages (see Hally 1983a), a number of unanswered questions remain. For example, why do some pots have an oxidized patch and others not? Why do the Kalinga pots get such a glossy soot layer, which on some vessels could be mistaken for purposeful smudging of the surface similar to some southwestern pottery types? And finally, why do worn-out pots (na-u-log) get an oxidized patch on the base? The experiments that follow are designed to clarify some of these questions and also to add to a general understanding of the process of pottery sooting.

Several variables in the sooting process were explored experimentally. These include how different woods (primarily softwoods and hardwoods) affect soot patterns, how the height over the fire influences soot deposition, and the role that moisture plays in soot and oxidation patterns. For the experiments both Kalinga-made vessels and laboratory-made pottery are used.

Sooting: Distance from Heat Source

As Hally's (1983a) experiments demonstrated, the distance of the ceramic vessel from the fire affects soot deposition. The critical variable is temperature: Different types of soot are deposited on surfaces of varying temperature. Temperature is discussed first because it is the most significant factor in soot deposition, and it may play a role in the two other factors (discussed later).

To explore how distance from the fire (i.e., temperature) affects sooting, experiments were done with a ceramic slab placed vertically in a fire. The slab was made with a clay that fires white (Westwood EM210) to enhance visually the zones of sooting. The slab was tempered heavily with sand and fired to 700° C. It measures 40 cm long, 29 cm wide, and about 9 mm thick. The experimental hearth consisted of a metal grate, about 10.2 cm above the ground, and two bricks (10.2 cm wide) to support the ceramic slab over the grate (Figure 7.4).

Figure 7.4. Setup for sooting experiment.

Three experiments were conducted, each consisting of either four 20-minute stages (softwood and hardwood) or two 20-minute stages (Kalinga wood) with the slab over the fire. Each experiment was identical except for the type of fuel used: softwood (Pinyon pine and Douglas fir), hardwood (pecan), and a Kalinga firewood (*Lapachik* and *Balbalasan*—both are softwoods). For each experiment, the slab was suspended over the fire as shown in Figure 7.4. The fuel was stacked so that it came as close to the the slab as possible without touching. During the burn, wood was continually added to insure that the fire burned as close to the bottom of the slab as possible. The fire was lit with a butane torch and as soon as the fire burned without assistance (less than a minute), timing began. After 20 minutes over the fire, the slab was removed and allowed to cool. The sooting patterns were recorded, and then the slab was lightly scrubbed with a paper towel and tap water. All removable soot was easily washed away, leaving the permanent soot layer. The sooting patterns were recorded, and the slab was again put over the fire. This process was repeated four times for each type of wood (except for the Kalinga wood—only two stages were performed). To remove the soot from the slab between experiments, it was heated in a kiln at 500° C (30-minute soak). All soot was removed and the slab regained its original appearance.

The results of the experimentation indicate that several types of soot are deposited on the ceramic. The first soot layer, which is created by all wood types, covers most of the ceramic slab soon after the fire is lit (Figure 7.5). It is a flat black, fluffy soot deposit that probably consists of coke, fragments of char, and ash (Medalia and Rivin 1982). This layer of soot can be removed easily with running water and light wiping. Because I am concerned only with soot that is permanently (relatively) affixed to the pottery surface, this layer is not considered further.

When the fluffy black soot is removed by washing, the second and third patches of soot are visible. The second patch occurs in an arc shape over the fire. This area is referred to as the oxidized patch because it is either completely white (no soot) or is slightly gray (Figure 7.6). In one case, there is both a completely oxidized patch and above that a gray patch. But regardless of the specific color, all slabs have an oxidized patch, or at least very reduced sooting at the point nearest to the fire. It is formed with all three wood types, and it is visible after the first 20-minute stage of the experiment.

Two things happen at the point of the oxidized patch. First, any soot on the surface or any organic matter in the clay will burn off. On the second through the fourth stages of each experiment, the oxidized area becomes sooted soon after the fire is started; but, as the ceramic becomes hot, the soot is again removed. Any organic matter in the clay would also burn off, possibly leaving a patch that would be lighter in color than the original ceramic surface (see Hally 1983a).

The second factor at work in the area of the oxidized patch is that the ceramic surface becomes so hot that no new soot will form. At

Figure 7.5. Ceramic slab becomes covered with flat-black, fluffy soot soon after the fire is lit.

roughly 10 minutes of each stage of the experiment, an oxidized patch began to form. After the area was initially sooted, the oxidized patch appeared as the temperature of the ceramic began to increase. In the laboratory kiln, by 400° C soot begins to burn off, so one could estimate that the ceramic surface is at least 400° C (and probably greater), which is well within the range of temperatures generated by open fires. To summarize, the temperature of the ceramic is so great right near the fire that (1) soot on the surface or organic matter in the clay will oxidize, and (2) no new soot will be deposited. This process is repeated during every

Figure 7.6. A sooted slab that shows the oxidized patch at the point closest to the fire.

heating episode; the ceramic surface is cool at first and becomes sooted, but as the temperature reaches 400° C the soot is oxidized.

The third patch of soot is a completely black, sometimes slightly lustrous layer that extends from the oxidized patch to nearly the top of the slab, about 30 to 40 cm from the base. This layer fades as the distance from the fire increases. These less dark layers to the top and side of the slab are not thought to be a different type of soot; they appear only to be less sooted and lighter in color because less soot has come in contact with the surface. As the duration of heating over a fire increases, this third layer of soot grows and completely blackens the experimental slabs. Although this layer has slightly different qualities depending upon the wood used (discussed later), it occurs in all experiments. It likely consists of coke, char fragments, and ash with the addition of carbon cenospheres. Carbon cenospheres are formed when liquid drops, drawn up by the rising gases, solidify on the pottery surface (Medalia and Rivin 1982:483). All soot that becomes permanently affixed to the ceramic is thought to contain these drops of carbonized resin.

One surprising finding of this sooting experiment is that the very glossy soot layer seen on the Kalinga pottery was not replicated, even with the Kalinga wood. That is because the resin droplets that solidify and are responsible for the glossy soot layer only appear on a relatively cool ceramic surface. Though other factors can contribute to the high glossy appearance of the soot, such as a very resinous wood or cool ceramic temperatures (e.g., from cool air temperature or a cool burning fire), the principal way to cool the pottery surface and permit the resin droplets to solidify is to fill the pot with water. The effect of moisture on sooting was also explored experimentally.

Sooting: The Role of Moisture

The possibility that moisture may play a role in pottery sooting was discovered by observing Kalinga pots that were *na-u-log,* worn out. In Kalinga, a pot is said to be *na-u-log* when it no longer will boil water or cooking of food takes too long. Kalinga cooks realize that this happens because the resin has worn away and the pot no longer has an interior water seal. Previous experiments (i.e., Schiffer 1990) have demonstrated that a pot with high water permeability is inefficient in heating its contents; some vessels of this kind were even incapable of bringing water to a boil. Kalinga pots that are *na-u-log* are intact and show no obvious signs of being unusable for cooking. The vessels are often reused for roasting coffee or for storing pig food. The only visible change in the pots occurs in the sooting pattern. As described earlier, *na-u-log* vessels often have an oxidized patch on the base that is bigger than on any functioning cooking vessel. The first set of experiments is designed to explore how water that permeates a vessel wall affects pottery sooting.

A second set of experiments explores how the sooting pattern is affected by water inside the vessel that does not permeate to the exterior surface. The previous experiments demonstrated how sooting is affected by the temperature of the ceramic surface, and the tests that follow explore how water in the pot changes the sooting pattern by lowering the pottery surface temperature.

The experiments employ previously unused Kalinga pots and the traditional Kalinga pot supports (Figure 7.7). The experiments conducted included (1) boiling water in a Kalinga pot (with interior resin) with both a softwood and hardwood fire; (2) boiling water in a Kalinga pot (without interior resin) in a softwood fire; and (3) sooting a Kalinga pot (with resin) that held no water. All pots used were of the Kalinga "everyday" size (3 to 4 chupas). In the experiments that involved water, pots were filled one-third with tap water, from 750 to 1000 ml depending on vessel size. In all cases, the pots were set on the pot supports so the vessel bottom was about 13 cm above the ground and about 3 to 5 cm above the wood. The fires were lit with a butane torch and wood was added as needed. Unless otherwise specified, the pots were sooted twice and washed with a paper towel and water after each heating episode. The pots were left on the fire until the water boiled, which was between 10 to 24 minutes. The pot without interior resin showed no signs of boiling, so after 22 minutes it was removed from the fire.

Figure 7.7. Setup for whole pot sooting experiment.

The results of these experiments demonstrate that moisture plays a role in sooting in two ways. First, water in the vessel cools the pottery surface and changes the type of soot that is deposited. The most significant changes are the absence of an oxidized patch, which requires very high temperatures, and more deposition of the glossy soot layer. The latter forms only when the surface of pottery is relatively cool; recall that very little glossy soot was formed on the ceramic slab. To illustrate how water cools the pottery surface and promotes a different pattern of soot deposition, it is instructive to look at vessels sooted under three different conditions. The first set of conditions (similar to those in the experiments that sooted the slab) was sooting a vessel, containing no water, in a hardwood fire for one 24-minute episode. The resultant sooting patterns on the vessel and the ceramic slab are also very similar. After washing, two sooted areas are visible: a slightly oxidized base (Figure 7.8), and from the lower exterior side to the rim there is a dark, predominantly nonglossy soot layer. Because there was no water in this vessel, the ceramic surface, especially at the base, gets very hot and promotes the formation of an oxidized patch. The hotter ceramic surface also reduces the formation of carbon cenospheres—liquid droplet carbonization. Fewer carbon cenospheres create a dull rather than glossy soot layer.

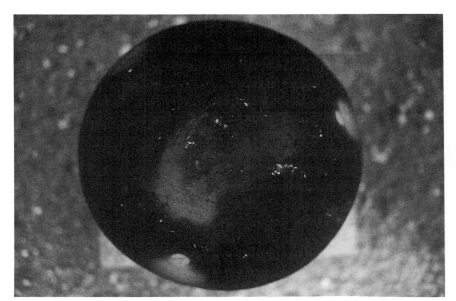

Figure 7.8. Base of a pot after sooting showing an oxidized patch.

The second set of conditions involved boiling water in a situation similar to what one would find in a Kalinga household. Water was boiled in two resin-coated pots; one with a hardwood fire and the other with a softwood fire. Each pot was kept on the fire until the water boiled—about 20 minutes for the softwood fire and about 10 minutes for the hardwood fire. Each pot was sooted twice. Despite the different wood and slightly varying conditions, the pots acquired a very similar sooting pattern. No oxidized patch occurs on the base, and slightly more of the glossy soot is formed (Figure 7.9). Under these conditions, the water in the vessel keeps the exterior surface cooler; this does not permit the base to get hot enough to oxidize, and the cooler surface promotes the carbonization of the liquid droplets.

The third set of conditions included heating water in a Kalinga pot that contained no interior resin. Softwood was used for two 20-minute sooting episodes. Without the interior resin, Kalinga pots are very permeable. In fact, moisture was visible on the exterior of the vessel soon after it was filled and throughout heating (Figure 7.10). The experiment was terminated after 22 minutes because the water was not near boiling. The glossy soot patch, after two sooting episodes, covers the base of the pot but stops abruptly at the level of the water during heating (Figure 7.11).

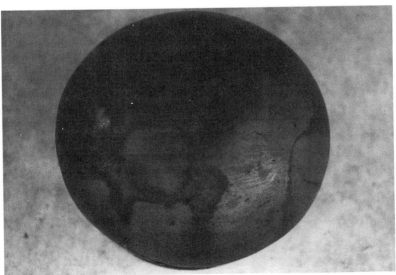

Figure 7.9. Resin-coated pot that was filled with water during sooting. Note the lack of an oxidized patch and the presence of glossy soot.

Figure 7.10. Water visible on the exterior of the vessel that does not have an interior coat of resin.

Above the water line, the more typical, less glossy soot can be found. In this case, the pottery surface below the water line was kept cool enough for a greater amount of liquid droplet carbonization, but the pottery surface above the water line remained hotter, which reduced the amount of liquid droplet carbonization.

In these three pots (no water, a pot with interior resin filled with water, and a pot without interior resin filled with water), there is a progression in sooting patterns that demonstrates the effect of moisture in cooling the ceramic surface. Different types of soot accumulate on ceramic surfaces of different temperatures. On the empty pot, the sooting pattern matches that found on the earlier experiments with the ceramic slabs. The surface of the pot is very hot, and there is little carbonization of the liquid droplets, and an oxidized patch forms on the base. When a pot has a resin coating and is filled with water, the sooting pattern is slightly different; because the vessel surface is cooler, there is more carbonization of liquid droplets (more of the glossy soot), and no oxidized patch appears. On the pot without resin, water permeates the vessel wall and keeps the surface of the pot relatively cool. This vessel is primarily covered with glossy soot.

Figure 7.11. Glossy soot occurs below the water level on a vessel without an interior coat of resin.

The second way that the sooting process is affected by water is if a relatively large amount of water permeates to the exterior surface. This process was discovered rather fortuitously while sooting a vessel with a hardwood fire. The vessel had an interior coating of resin and was filled with about 750 ml of water. After about 20 minutes heating, it became apparent that the water was not going to boil, and the experiment was terminated. Evidently the pot had a hairline crack, not sealed with resin, that was permitting the water to travel rapidly to the surface. On closer inspection it was found that there are a number of small areas on the interior of the vessel that did not get covered with resin. On this pot, the water was interfering with heating, in a manner similar to the vessel with no resin coating. The result is an unusual but revealing sooting pattern.

At the point of the crack where water was escaping to the exterior surface there is a small patch that is completely oxidized (Figure 7.12a). Apparently the water turning to steam did not permit the formation of soot. Surrounding this small oxidized patch and on several other areas is glossy soot similar to the deposits on the vessels with no resin (Figure 7.12b). The sooting pattern on this vessel demonstrates

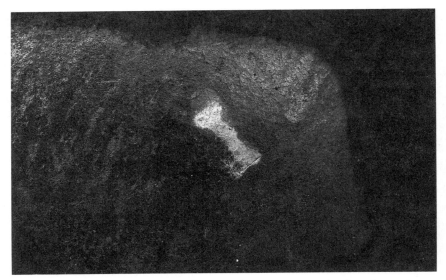

Figure 7.12a. A small oxidized patch occurs where water was seeping through a crack.

two things. First, if water is present in sufficient amounts to actually vaporize on the surface, no soot will be deposited. A similar process may be responsible for the oxidized patch on the *na-u-log* pots. Second, the cooler surface not only permits the carbonization of the liquid drops but in some cases will inhibit the formation of the fluffy soot layer seen on all pots thus far (i.e., the sooting pattern seen in Figure 12a and 12b could be seen before washing). It is likely that in this case, there is so much liquid droplet carbonization that it seals the fluffy soot layer to the ceramic surface.

Sooting: The Effect of Wood Type

All wood consists of varying amounts, depending on wood species, of cellulose, hemicellulose, and lignin. At the most general level, softwoods (coniferous) have more lignin, which is the glue that holds wood together, and hardwoods (deciduous) have more cellulose and hemicellulose, which are the carbohydrates (Tillman *et al.* 1981:18-34). Moreover, hardwoods generally have a lower moisture content than softwoods. Combustion of wood proceeds through four stages: (1) heating and drying, (2) solid particle pyrolysis, (3) gas phase pyrolysis, and (4) char

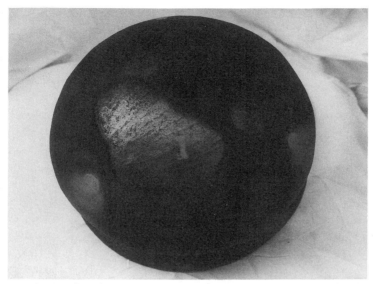

Figure 7.12b. The effect of moisture on sooting. A small oxidized patch occurs near the crack, and glossy soot is deposited on the cooler area of the vessel.

formation. Both the chemical composition and moisture content affect the reaction of wood in these four stages (for a complete discussion, see Tillman *et al.* 1981). One of the most important factors is that softwoods (because of greater amounts of lignin) can generate more heat (Tillman 1978:67-68), but higher moisture levels of wood will reduce combustion efficiency. To explore the effect of different woods on the deposition of soot on ceramic, I refer again to the experimental sooting of the ceramic slabs.

The effect of wood type on pottery sooting is complex. The experiment that follows is only a pilot study that begins to explore the basic difference between the sooting of pottery with a hardwood and softwood fire.

The ceramic slab (refer to the earlier section for a description of its dimensions, composition, and methods of manufacture) was sooted by burning three types of wood: hardwood (pecan), softwood (Pinyon pine and Douglas fir), and Kalinga softwoods (*Balbalasan* and *Lapachik*). One sooting episode consisted of 20 minutes over the fire (see previous discussion for a description of experimental procedures), and the slab was sooted for four episodes in a hardwood and softwood fire but only twice using the Kalinga wood. This did not seem to be a significant adjustment in procedures (made necessary by a shortage of Kalinga wood) because in all cases the sooting patterns had reached a plateau by the second episode.

The most significant result of this experiment is that all wood types produce similar sooting patterns: (1) a primary soot layer (that washes away), presumed to consist of coke and char fragments; (2) the oxidized patch near the base of the slab; and (3) the permanent soot layer thought to be composed primarily of carbon cenospheres mixed with coke and char fragments. The only real difference in the sooting pattern that can be seen with the naked eye occurs on the slab sooted in the Kalinga wood fire.

Two differences appear on the slabs sooted by combustion of Kalinga wood. The first is the size of the oxidized patch (Figure 7.13). The slab sooted with a Kalinga wood fire has a larger oxidized patch then either the slabs sooted with either the hardwood or softwood fires (which have similar-size oxidized patches). Compare the size of the oxidized patch in Figure 7.6 to Figure 7.13. The larger area of oxidization on the slab produced by the combustion of Kalinga wood suggests that the heat produced by the fire was greater than either the soft or hardwood fires. Presumably this is because the Kalinga wood has greater amounts of lignin. The softwood used in this experiment should also have greater amounts of lignin than the hardwood, but this was not evident in the sooting patterns.

The second difference in sooting patterns is that the Kalinga wood fire produced a larger and blacker primary soot deposit. This layer is thought to be composed of coke and char fragments as a result of incomplete combustion. The reason for the greater amount of primary soot is not known, but for this study it is of less importance because this layer of soot would not be permanently affixed to the pottery surface.

This pilot study has informed us about several points important in pottery sooting. Regardless of the type of wood, a basic sooting pattern will develop on a pottery surface. All produced a hot enough flame to form an oxidized patch and above this region, the combustion of all three wood types produced a layer of soot that was visually similar and was composed, presumably, of coke char fragments, ash, and carbonized liquid drops of resin.

But this preliminary experiment also demonstrated that the combustion of different wood types can produce some differences in sooting. The

Figure 7.13. The larger oxidized patch on the slab sooted by the burning of Kalinga wood.

Kalinga wood fire produced a bigger oxidized patch and a darker and larger primary soot layer (i.e., the soot that washes off). It is anticipated, however, that other factors such as dryness of the wood and draft in the hearth are just as important in soot formation as wood type.

DISCUSSION AND SUMMARY

Carbon deposits on the interior and exterior of pottery can provide information on what was cooked, how it was cooked, and the overall position of the vessel over the fire. Kalinga vegetable/meat and rice cooking pots can be distinguished based on both the interior and exterior carbon deposits. Interior carbon deposits, caused by the charring of food particles, can provide information on the source and intensity of heat and also something about the cooking process. Although all Kalinga cooking pots tended to have similar interior carbon deposits, it was found that they were formed by different processes. There is a tendency to have a patch of carbon on the interior base and a ring of carbon on the midinterior side. It was determined, by recording carbon deposits on vessels used for varying lengths of time and by observing pots in use, that interior carbon deposits on the midinterior side of vegetable/meat and rice cooking pots were formed by very different processes. The patch of carbon that rings the midinterior side of the vegetable/meat cooking pots is formed at the top of the water level as food particles, floating on the water, adhere and become carbonized on the pottery surface. The carbon patch in the same area on the rice cooking pots is formed as the pots sit in the simmer position at the side of the fire. The side of the pot while in this position is subject to high heat and, as the water is removed, the rice chars and adheres to the pottery surface. A similar process is responsible for the thermal spalls and oxidized patch on the midinterior side.

If nothing was known about Kalinga cooking, one could make several inferences based only on interior carbon deposits. The carbonized patch on the base suggests that both the vegetable/meat and rice cooking pots were suspended over the fire. Moreover, one could also infer that rice cooking pots are set next to a source of heat at some point during cooking. The interior patch of carbon on the midinterior side of the vegetable/meat pots would suggest that food is boiled and that the pots are filled with water to about the midpoint.

The exterior carbon deposits (or soot) are also correlated with the mode of cooking. All cooking vessels have basically the same sooting pattern, suggesting that both the vegetable/meat and rice cooking pots are subject to similar cooking practices. The thinner patch of soot (and sometimes oxidized patch) on the base suggests that all cooking pots are set above the source of heat. The oxidized spots found on many rice cooking pots suggest that they were set next to the source of heat. But there were several questions about sooting generated by the Kalinga study that needed to be addressed experimentally. These include why some pots have an oxidized patch and others do not; why Kalinga pots have such a highly glossy soot layer; and why worn-out pots get an oxidized patch on the base? Other experiments in this study suggest that Kalinga pots are set on the hearth at a height above the fire that puts them at the border between the oxidized and sooted patch. Some Kalinga pots, therefore, get an oxidized patch, and others do not. The glossy soot layer on the Kalinga pottery is caused by excessive liquid drop carbonization. The experiments demonstrated that this form of soot is deposited only on cool ceramic surfaces caused, in the Kalinga case, by water in the vessels. The highly resinous wood used in Kalinga hearths may also contribute to the glossy soot.

The final question addressed by the experiments (why does the oxidized patch form on the exterior base of worn-out pots?) was not answered completely. In the experiments, it was found that if a great deal of water permeates the surface, no soot will accumulate. This could be a factor in the formation of the oxidized patches on the *na-u-log* pots. But the pot in the experiment with no interior resin did not get an oxidized patch, only more carbonization of liquid drops. Possibly, the hotter fires produced by the Kalinga wood play a role in this process. It is also possible that the Kalinga cooks are required to leave the *na-u-log* pots on the fire much longer because the permeating water greatly interferes with its heating effectiveness. The longer period on the fire, possibly made bigger to get the water to boil, may create the larger oxidized patch. After the cook has such a difficult time bringing the water to boil in that cooking episode, the pot is determined to be *na-u-log*, and it is retired, with an oxidized patch on the base, from active duty as a cooking pot.

As this study demonstrates, archaeologists can now make more refined inferences about cooking based upon interior and exterior carbon deposition. Although determining whether a pot was or was not used for cooking is a fundamental and important inference, much more can now be said about what was cooked and the actual activities involved in cooking. Further implications of this research are discussed in the concluding chapter.

Chapter *8*
Concluding Comments

In the preceding pages, I discuss how *actual* pottery use can be determined from traces mapped onto vessels. Using ethnoarchaeological and experimental data, this study investigated the processes that govern the formation of organic residues, carbon deposits, and surface attrition. These three forms of pottery use alteration can inform directly on how pottery was used, which is critical to many archaeological inferences.

Despite the importance of knowing actual pottery function in archaeological inference, little is known about pottery use in everyday life. How is household size inferred from cooking pot attributes without the ability to isolate daily-use cooking vessels from other pots in a household assemblage? Can a complete picture be formed of prehistoric diet when little is known about what was prepared in cooking vessels? Is it possible to understand the meaning of pottery designs if there is no accurate information about pottery function? Can archaeologists really understand technological and stylistic change without knowing how pottery was used in everyday life? These questions underscore the utility of reconstructing actual pottery use. The research presented in this study is the first comprehensive investigation of pottery use alteration—the only approach for determining *actual* pottery use. This research provides the core of information necessary for archaeologists to perform use-alteration analyses on their pottery assemblage. What is needed now are use-alteration case studies on prehistoric pottery assemblages.

In order to both review and evaluate this use-alteration study, two questions are addressed: (1) What does the Kalinga case study tell us about the pottery use-alteration analysis in archaeology? and (2) Can archaeologists now begin to employ rigorously use-alteration studies to determine pottery use?

The first question can be answered by highlighting a number of findings of the Kalinga study. The first is that clear and consistent use-alteration patterns can be discerned. All three forms of use alteration (carbon deposition, surface attrition, and residues) formed consistent patterns on Kalinga pots. Based on each form of use alteration, pots used for rice cooking could be distinguished from those for vegetable/ meat cooking.

Second, a general use-alteration framework was developed that (1) distinguished traces produced by use and those not produced by use (e.g., in a depositional context), and (2) defined the three major types of use alteration (carbon deposition, residues, and attrition). Other studies have employed one or sometimes two forms of use alteration, but this study demonstrates that all three forms of use alteration provide important and different information.

Third, this case study set the parameters of the three forms of use alteration: the activities that can and cannot be determined from surface attrition, carbon deposition, and absorbed residues. Surface attrition can provide information about activities such as washing, stirring, carrying, and storing. In some cases, as in thermal spalling, surface attrition provides information about how the vessel was heated as well. But the Kalinga case study also demonstrated that some activities are not recorded as attritional traces. Some actions were simply not abrasive enough to cause significant surface modification, and others were obliterated by other surface traces.

Absorbed residues, in this case fatty acids, provide information about what was stored or cooked in the vessel. In the Kalinga case study, rice cooking pots could be distinguished from vegetable/meat cooking pots. One limitation of this technique is that it is difficult to identify individual plant or animal species if the pot was used to cook many items. In several Kalinga pots, it could be said that meat was cooked, but none of the vegetables could be identified. It was also found that hydrolysis and oxidation will change and break down fatty acids under certain conditions.

Interior and exterior carbon deposits provide information about what was cooked and how it was cooked. Interior carbon is created by charring of food and is governed by the source and intensity of heat and the presence of moisture. Exterior carbon (or soot) can yield information about the position of the pot over the fire, the intensity of the fire, the contents of the pot, and the permeability of the vessel wall.

Tables 8.1-8.4 illustrate how different use-alteration traces can be used to infer different components of a pottery use activity. Recall that there are five components of any pottery use activity. For each activity that is illustrated (cooking, cleaning, transport, and storage), a different set of use-alteration traces can be applied. One should note that attrition is the richest use-alteration trace in that it can potentially inform about all five components of an activity in all four of the pottery use activities illustrated (Tables 8.1-8.4). An archaeologist who attempts a pottery use-alteration study must be aware of which use activities (and which component of each activity) is of interest and then concentrate on use-alteration traces that are most appropriate.

The fourth and final finding of the Kalinga case study was the importance of a combined experimental and ethnoarchaeological approach. The key to pottery use alteration is understanding the processes that govern the production of use traces. This study would not have been completely possible without combining ethnoarchaeological observations of pottery use and experimentation. To develop the parameters of use alteration and to understand the processes that govern the production of traces, it was important to observe pottery use in an ethnoarchaeological setting. Experiments build upon ethnoarchaeological data in two ways. First, no one ethnoarchaeological data set will produce every use-alteration pattern. Experiments can expand one's knowledge of use-alteration trace production by replicating various use behaviors. Second, experiments, because of the greater control of variables, can be more readily used to explore the process of trace production. The experiments in this study were performed to understand the processes of soot deposition. A number of experiments on ceramic abrasion were also performed earlier (e.g., Skibo 1987; Skibo and Schiffer 1987; Vaz Pinto *et al.* 1987). These experiments provided the framework for exploring the relationship between abrader, ceramic, and action.

The second question introduced before is: Can archaeologists now begin to employ use-alteration studies to determine pottery use? In a word, yes. In this study, the objective was first to identify the forms of use alteration and then to understand the processes involved in their

Table 8.1. Use-Alteration Traces and Components of Cooking Activity[a]

Components of use activity	Organic residue	Carbon deposits		Attrition	
		Interior	Exterior	Interior	Exterior
User characteristics	−	−	−	+	+
Context	−	+	+	+	+
Actions	−	+	+	+	+
Time/frequency	+	+	+	+	+
Contents	+	+	−	+	+

[a]The pluses and minuses illustrate whether a use-alteration trace can potentially inform on that component of cooking.

formation. An archaeologist, armed with the principles of use-alteration formation, should be able to determine various aspects of pottery use. To illustrate the process of combining use-alteration traces to infer vessel function, one Kalinga pottery type—the *ittoyom/oppaya*—is now analyzed briefly.

The people of Guina-ang recognize a pottery type that is not easily put into the formal Kalinga cooking pot categories. Based on morphological features they refer to such a pot as an "*ittoyom/oppaya*" and say that they will use the pot for cooking rice or vegetables and meat. There were 66 *ittoyom/oppaya* in Guina-ang households at the time of our research. It is interesting that not all of these pots were used to cook both rice and vegetable/meat. Of all the *ittoyom/oppaya* that were used to cook vegetable/meat, rice, or both, 17 were used for vegetable/meat cooking, 18 were used for rice cooking, and 16 were said to be used for both.

Table 8.2. Use-Alteration Traces and Components of Cleaning Activity[a]

Components of use activity	Organic residue	Carbon deposits		Attrition	
		Interior	Exterior	Interior	Exterior
User characteristics	−	−	−	+	+
Context	−	−	−	+	+
Actions	−	−	−	+	+
Time/frequency	−	−	−	+	+
Contents	NA	NA		NA	

[a]The pluses and minuses illustrate whether a use-alteration trace can potentially inform on that component of pottery cleaning.

Table 8.3. Use-Alteration Traces and Components of Storage Activity[a]

	Pottery storage				
		Use-alteration traces			
Components of use activity	Organic residue	Carbon deposits		Attrition	
		Interior	Exterior	Interior	Exterior
User characteristics	−	−	−	+	+
Context	−	−	−	−	+
Actions	−	−	−	+	+
Time/frequency	+	−	−	+	+
Contents	+	−	−	+	+

[a]The pluses and minuses illustrate whether a use-alteration trace can potentially inform on that component of pottery storage.

These data were collected during interviews and relied on the memory of the informants. The use-alteration information demonstrates that informants were usually correct; use-alteration traces usually confirm the informant responses about vessel use. But use-alteration traces on one vessel (H23P17) suggest that the informant was in error.

This *ittoyom/oppaya* (H23P17) was said to be used only for cooking vegetables and meat, but carbon deposition and surface attrition demonstrate that it was also used for cooking rice. The interior is abraded and pitted, suggesting that it did see use as a vegetable/meat cooking pot. But the midinterior side also has thermal spalls, suggesting that it did spend time in the simmer position during the final stage of rice cooking. Moreover, there are carbonized patches on the midinterior side that confirm that the pot was placed in the simmer position. In Kalinga households, only rice cooking pots acquire these two traces.

Table 8.4. Use-Alteration Traces and Components of Pottery Transport[a]

	Pottery transport				
		Use-alteration traces			
Components of use activity	Organic residue	Carbon deposits		Attrition	
		Interior	Exterior	Interior	Exterior
User characteristics	−	−	−	+	+
Context	−	−	−	+	+
Actions	−	−	−	+	+
Time/frequency	−	−	−	+	+
Contents	NA	NA		NA	

[a]The pluses and minuses illustrate whether a use-alteration trace can potentially inform on that component of pottery transport.

This brief example demonstrates the advantages of a use-alteration analysis. Use-alteration traces are more accurate than interview data; the former record actual use, not intended or presumed use. Moreover, this example shows that different use-alteration traces (when combined) can yield information about use not obtainable elsewhere. In this case, the residue data from the *ittoyom/oppaya* would likely be indeterminate; roughly equal numbers of these vessels are used to cook rice, vegetable/meat, or both. The morphological attributes would also provide nothing conclusive about use because *ittoyom/oppaya* do not fit neatly into either of the cooking pot categories. Finally, this example illustrates that pottery use can be inferred when there is no (or in this case incorrect) evidence about how the vessel was actually used.

A FINAL COMMENT

Ceramics are unique archaeological data; they break and are manufactured often, they are very resistant to postdepositional breakdown, and people often produce pottery to fulfill functions (techno-, socio-, and ideofunctions). As a result, ceramic data are often the source for many archaeological inferences. Nearly any inference based on pottery, however, must have information about pottery use—how the pots functioned in everyday life. Traces of pottery use, in the form of alterations to the ceramic, provide the only evidence of *actual* use. In this work, I show that surface attrition, absorbed residues, and carbon deposition can be linked to pottery use. Residues provide information on what was stored or cooked, attrition reveals how the pot was manipulated during use, and carbon deposits provide evidence for what was cooked and how it was heated. These use-alteration traces, when combined, can lead to more precise inferences about actual pottery function.

In the introductory chapter, I mentioned that the task for the archaeologist is not easy. Understanding the relationship between material culture and behavior is difficult in its own right, but archaeologists must accomplish this feat with only fragmentary items—literally reconstructing the puzzle with only a few pieces. Pottery use alteration, by providing direct evidence of pottery use, is one method that can make this task easier.

Appendix *A*

Data Collection Forms

Household inventory
(Example)

Village: *Guina-ang*
Page *1* of *4*

Household no. *One*
Family name: *Dayag*
Date: *April 18, 1988*

Pot no.	Type	Gili	Where made/ Potter name	Relationship	Where and when/ How obtained
1	Ittoyom Small		Dangtalan/ Chamaya	None	Guina-ang, 1987 Bartered

Pottery measurements
(Example)

Page 2 of 4

Household no. *One*

Pot no.	Size (chupas)	Height	Circumference	Neck diameter	Aperture
1	4	15 cm	74 cm	18 cm	22 cm

Pottery use questionnaire
(Example)

Household no. *One*   Pot no. *One*

1. When was the pot last used? *April 16, 1988*
2. What is the pot now used for? *Cook rice*
3. (ITTOYOM ONLY) Is the pot ever used as an *oppaya*? *No*
4. (OPPAYA ONLY) Is the pot ever used to cook rice? ___
5. How much soot (none, little, heavy, chipping)? *Heavy*
6. Is there an oxidized patch on the base? *No*
7. Does the pot leak? *No*
8. Is the rim chipped? *Yes*
9. Is the pot cracked? *No*
10. Has the pot been repaired? *No*
11. List the pots used during the last Breakfast: *Pot 6, Pot 2*
                                              Lunch: *Pot 6, Pot 1*
                                              Dinner: *Pot 3, Pot 1*
12. Is a metal pot used for cooking rice (always, sometimes, or never)? *Sometimes*
13. Is a metal pot used to cook vegetable/meat? *Never*
14. List all household pot washers and give age. *Housewife, daughter (5 years old)*
15. Is a metal or coconut ladle used? *Both*
16. Is a metal or wood rice spatula used? *Wood*
17. Does the house have a metal, ceramic, or stone hearth support? *Ceramic*
18. Which village makes the best water jars? *Dalupa*
    Why? *Well polished, available*
19. Which village makes the best cooking pots? *Dangtalan*
    Why? *More durable*

Fatty Acid Identification

with Jeffrey J. Clark

After the samples were prepared as outlined in Chapter 5, they were derivatized to their corresponding methyl esters. This facilitated their passage through the GC column. The samples were analyzed at the University of Arizona's Mass Spectrometry Facility. For those unfamiliar with gas chromatography/mass spectroscopy (GC/MS), the gas chromatograph separates the sample into its chemical compounds. The mass spectrometry identifies these compounds by measuring the relative amounts of degradation products of these compounds after bombardment with electrons. These degradation elements are separated by their atomic masses and are used as fingerprints to identify the structure of the parent compound through statistical correlation with a computer library of mass spectrographs of known compounds.

More specifically, our analysis used a Hewlett Packard 5980 gas chromatograph and a Hewlett Packard 5970 mass spectrograph. The column support for the GC that performed the isolation of individual fatty acids was a Hewlett Packard Ultra-2 (25 m in length and 0.2 mm in internal diameter). As is common with GC work, a temperature program was used to heat the GC oven that houses the column. The program utilized in our sample runs started with a column temperature of 70° C and was raised at a rate of 15° C/min until the temperature of 300° C was reached. The retention times of the isolated elements found on the chromatograph reflect a 1-minute delay from sample injection that allows the solvent peak to move through the column without being recorded. Actual mass spectrograms were recorded for all compounds that had a column retention time of over 4 minutes because no fatty acids could move through the column before this time. This shortens the time and length of analysis because there are numerous volatiles that elute off the GC column that are trivial to our analysis. The GC-isolated compounds were then analyzed by using standard mass spectrometry techniques.

References

Adams, William H.
1973   An ethnoarchaeological study of a rural American community: Silcott, Washington, 1900-1930. *Ethnohistory* 20:335-346.

Allen, Jim
1984   Pots and poor princes: A multidimensional approach to the role of pottery trading in coastal Papua. In *The many dimensions of pottery,* edited by S. E. van der Leeuw and H. C. Pritchard, pp. 407-463. University of Amsterdam Press, Amsterdam.

Arnold, Dean E.
1983   Design structure and community organization in Quinua, Peru. In *Structure and cognition in art,* edited by D. Washburn, pp. 56-73. Cambridge University Press, New York.

1985   *Ceramic theory and cultural process.* Cambridge University Press, New York.

Aronson, Meredith, James M. Skibo, and Miriam Stark
n.d.   Production and use technologies in Kalinga pottery. In *Kalinga ethnoarchaeology,* edited by W. A. Longacre and J. M. Skibo. Smithsonian Institution, Washington, D.C. (in press).

Ascher, Robert
1961a   Experimental archaeology. *American Anthropologist* 63:793-816.

1961b   Analogy in archaeological interpretation. *Southwestern Journal of Anthropology* 17:317-325.

Aurand, Leonard W., A. Edwin Woods, and Marion R. Wells
1987   *Food composition and analysis.* Van Nostrand Reinhold, New York.

Bacdayan, Albert S.
1967   *The peace pact system of the Kalingas in the modern world.* Ph.D. dissertation, Cornell University.

Barton, Roy F.
1949   *The Kalingas: Their institutions and custom law.* University of Chicago Press, Chicago.

Bennett, John W.
1943   Recent developments in the functional interpretation of archaeological data. *American Antiquity* 9:208-219.

Biers, William R., and Patrick E. McGovern (editors)
1990   Organic contents and ancient vessels: Materials analysis and archaeological investigation. In *MASCA Research Papers in Science and Archaeology, Vol 7.* The University of Pennsylvania, Philadelphia.

Binford, Lewis, R.
1962   Archaeology as anthropology. *American Antiquity* 28:217-225.
1965   Archaeological systematics and the study of culture process. *American Antiquity* 31:203-210.
1967   Smudge pits and hide smoking: The use of analogy in archaeological reasoning. *American Antiquity* 32:1-12.
1968   Archeological perspectives. In *New perspectives in archeology*, edited by S. R. Binford and L. R. Binford, pp. 5-32. Aldine, Chicago.
1978   *Nunamiut ethnoarchaeology.* Academic Press, New York.
1981   *Bones: Ancient men and modern myths.* Academic Press, New York.
1984a   Butchering, sharing, and the archaeological record. *Journal of Anthropological Archaeology* 3:235-257.
1984b   An Alyawara day: Flour, spinifex gum, and shifting perspectives. *Journal of Anthropological Research* 40:157-182
1985   "Brand X" versus the recommended product. *American Antiquity* 50:580-590.
1987   Researching ambiguity: Frames of reference and site structure. In *Method and theory for activity area research: An ethnoarchaeological approach,* edited by S. Kent, pp. 449-512. Columbia University Press, New York.

Blinman, Eric
1988   The interpretation of ceramic variability: A case study from the Dolores Anasazi. Ph.D. dissertation, Washington State University, Pullman.

Bowers, P. M., R. Bonnichsen, and D. M. Hoch
1983   Flake dispersal experiments: Noncultural transformation of the archaeological record. *American Antiquity* 48:553-572.

Braun, David
1980   Experimental interpretation of ceramic vessel use on the basis of rim and neck formal attributes, Appendix I. In *The Navajo Project,* edited by D. C. Fiero, R. W. Munson, M. T. McClain, S. M. Wilson, and A. H. Zier, pp. 171-231. *Museum of Northern Arizona, Research Paper 11.*
1983   Pots as tools. In *Archaeological hammers and theories,* edited by A. Keene and J. Moore, pp. 107-134. Academic Press, New York.

Braverman, J. B. S.
1963   *Introduction to the biochemistry of foods.* Elsevier, New York.

Bray, Alicia
1982   Mimbres Black-on-White, Melamine or Wedgewood [sic]? A ceramic use-wear analysis. *The Kiva* 47:133-151.

Bronitsky, Gordon
1986   The use of materials science techniques in the study of pottery construction and use. In *Advances in archaeological method and theory,* Volume 9, edited by M. B. Schiffer, pp. 209-276. Academic Press, Orlando.

Bronitsky, Gordon, and R. Hamer
1986   Experiments in ceramic technology: The effects of various tempering materials on impact and thermal shock resistance. *American Antiquity* 51:89-101.

Brown, Marley, III
1973   The use of oral and documentary sources in historical archaeology: Ethnohistory at the Mott Farm. *Ethnohistory* 20:347-360.

Buko, Andrzej
1990   The use of pottery erosion in the analysis of the processes of settlement site formation. *Sprawozdania Archeologiczne* 42:349-359 (in Polish).

Cackette, M. J., M. D'Auria, and Bryan E. Snow
  1987   Examining earthenware vessel function by elemental phosphorous content. *Current An-*
          thropology 28:121-127.

Carrasco y Perez, Telesforo
  1986   *A Spaniard in Aguinaldo's army* (translated by Nick Joaquin). Solar Publishing, Manila,
          Philippines.

Chang, Kwang-Chih
  1958   Study of the Neolithic social grouping: Examples from the New World. *American Anthro-*
          pologist 60:298-334.

Chernela, J.
  1969   In praise of the scratch: The importance of aboriginal abrasion on museum ware. *Curator*
          12:174-179.

Christie, William W.
  1989   *Gas chromatography and lipids: A practical guide.* The Oily Press, Ayr, Scotland.

Claassen, Cheryl P.
  1981   Experimentation with model materials. In *Modern material culture studies: The archaeology*
          of us, edited by R. A. Gould and M. B. Schiffer, pp. 239-246. Academic Press, New York.

Coles, John
  1973   *Archaeology by experiment.* Charles Scribner's Sons, New York.
  1979   *Experimental archaeology.* Academic Press, New York.

Condamin, J., F. Formenti, M. O. Metais, M. Michel, and P. Blond
  1976   The application of gas chromatography to the tracing of oil in ancient amphorae.
          Archaeometry 18:195-201.

Cordell, Linda S.
  1991   Anna O. Shepard and southwestern archaeology: Ignoring a cautious heretic. In *The ce-*
          ramic legacy of Anna O. Shepard, edited by R. L. Bishop and F. W. Lange, pp. 132-153.
          University of Colorado Press, Boulder.

Crown, Patricia L.
  1991   Appraising the legacy: A thematic synthesis. In *The ceramic legacy of Anna O. Shepard,*
          edited by R. L. Bishop and F. W. Lange, pp. 383-393. Unviversity of Colorado Press,
          Boulder.

Cushing, Frank H.
  1886   A study of pueblo pottery as illustrative of Zuni culture growth. *4th Annual Report of the*
          Bureau of Ethnology, 1882-1883, pp. 473-521. Smithsonian Institution Press, Washington,
          D.C.
  1894   Primitive copper working: An experimental study. *American Anthropologist* 7:93-117.

David, N., and H. Henning
  1972   The ethnography of pottery: A Fulani case seen in archaeological perspective. *Addison-*
          Wesley Module in Anthropology, 21.

Deal, Michael
  n.d.   The role of ceramics among the prehistoric hunter-gatherers of the Maine-Maritime re-
          gion: A residue approach. In *Prehistoric archaeology in the Maritimes: Past and present re-*
          search, edited by M. Deal (in press). Council of Maritime Premiers, Federation.
  1982   Functional variation in Maya spiked vessels: A practical guide. *American Antiquity* 47:614-
          633.
  1983   *Pottery ethnoarchaeology among the Tzeltal Maya.* Ph.D. dissertation, Simon Fraser Univer-
          sity, Burnaby, British Columbia.
  1985   Household pottery disposal in the Maya Highlands: An ethnoarchaeological interpreta-
          tion. *Journal of Anthropological Archaeology* 4:243-291.

1990   Exploratory analysis of food residues from prehistoric pottery and other artifacts from eastern Canada. *Society for Archaeological Sciences Bulletin* 13(1):6-12.

Deal, Michael, and Peter Silk

1988   Absorption residues and vessel function: A case study from the Maine-Maritimes region. In *A pot for all reasons: Ceramic ecology revisited,* edited by C. C. Kolb and L. M. Lackey, pp. 105-125. Laboratory of Anthropology, Temple University, Philadelphia.

de Barros, P. L. F.

1982   The effects of variable site occupation span on the results of frequency seriation. *American Antiquity* 47:291-315.

De Atley, Suzanne P., and Ronald L. Bishop

1991   Toward an integrated interface for archaeology and archaeometry. In *The ceramic legacy of Anna O. Shepard,* edited by R. L. Bishop and F. W. Lange, pp. 358-380. University of Colorado Press, Boulder.

DeBoer, Warren R., and Donald W. Lathrap

1979   The making and breaking of Shipibo-Conibo ceramics. In *Ethnoarchaeology: Implications of ethnography for archaeology,* edited by C. Kramer, pp. 102-138. Columbia University Press, New York.

Deetz, James D. F.

1965   The dynamics of stylistic change in Arikara ceramics. *Illinois studies in anthropology, No. 4.* University of Illinois Press, Urbana.

DeGarmo, Glen Dean

1975   *Coyote Creek, Site 01: A methodological study of a prehistoric pueblo population.* Ph.D. dissertation, Department of Anthropology, University of California, Los Angeles.

DeNiro, M. J.

1987   Stable isotopy and archaeology. *American Scientist* 75:182-191.

De Raedt, Jules

1989   *Kalinga sacrifice.* Cordillera Studies Center, University of the Philippines, Baguio.

Dillon, Brian D.

1984   Ethnoarchaeology in Middle America: An introduction. *Journal of New World Archaeology* 6(2):1-3.

Donnan, Christopher B., and C. William Clewlow, Jr. (editors)

1974a   "Ethnoarchaeology." *Institute of Archaeology Monograph IV.* University of California, Los Angeles.

1974b   Introduction: A perspective on ethnoarchaeology. In "Ethnoarchaeology," edited by C. B. Donnan and C. W. Clewlow, Jr., pp. i-ii. *Institute of Archaeology Monograph IV.* University of California, Los Angeles.

Dozier, Edward P.

1966   *Mountain arbiters: The changing life of a Philippine hill people.* University of Arizona Press, Tucson.

Duma, G.

1972   Phosphate content of ancient pots as an indication of use. *Current Anthropology* 13:127-129.

Dunnell, R. C., and T. L. Hunt

1990   Elemental composition and inference of ceramic vessel function. *Current Anthropology* 31:330-336.

Ericson, Jonathan E., and Suzanne P. De Atley

1976   Reconstructing ceramic assemblages: An experiment to derive the morphology and capacity of parent vessels from sherds. *American Antiquity* 41:484-489.

Ericson, Jonathan E., Dwight Read, and Cheryl Burke
  1972   Research design: The relationship between primary function and the physical properties of ceramic vessels. *Anthropology UCLA* 3:84-95.

Evans, Margaret, Irene Vithanadurage, and Alan Williams
  1981   An investigation of the combustion of wood. *Journal of the Institute of Energy* 54:179-186.

Evans, W. E. D.
  1963   *The chemistry of death.* Charles C Thomas, Springfield.

Fenner, Gloria J.
  1977   Flare-rimmed bowls: A sub-type of Mimbres Classic Black-on-White? *The Kiva* 43:129-141.

Fewkes, Jesse W.
  1900   Tusayan migration traditions. *Bureau of American Ethnology Report for 1897-1898* 19:577-633.

Fish, Paul R.
  1978   Consistency in archaeological measurement and classification: A pilot study. *American Antiquity* 43:86-89.

Flannery, Kent V.
  1973   Archaeology with a capital S. In *Research and theory in current archeology,* edited by C. L. Redman, pp. 47-53. Wiley and Sons, New York.

Food and composition tables for the Near East
  1982   *FAO food and nutrition paper 26.* Food and Agriculture Organization of the United Nations, Rome.

Foster, George M.
  1960   Life-expectancy of utilitarian pottery in Tzintzuntzan, Michoacan, Mexico. *American Antiquity* 25:606-609.

Fourcroy
  1790   *Annales de Chimie* 5:154.

Gifford-Gonzalez, Diane P., David B. Damrosch, Debra R. Damrosch, John Pryor, and Robert L. Thunen
  1985   The third dimension in site structure: An experiment in trampling and vertical dispersal. *American Antiquity* 50:803-818.

Goldberg, Edward D.
  1985   *Black carbon in the environment: Properties and distribution.* John Wiley and Sons, New York.

Gould, Richard A.
  1971   The archaeologist as ethnographer: A case from the Western desert of Australia. *World Archaeology* 2:143-177.
  1980   *Living archaeology.* Cambridge University Press, Cambridge.
  1985   The empiricist strikes back: Reply to Binford. *American Antiquity* 50:638-644.

Gould, Richard A., and Michael B. Schiffer (editors)
  1981   *Modern material culture studies: The archaeology of us.* Academic Press, New York.

Gould, Richard A., and Patty Jo Watson
  1982   A dialogue on the meaning and use of analogy in ethnoarchaeological reasoning. *Journal of Anthropological Archaeology* 1:355-381.

Graves, Michael
  1981   *Ethnoarchaeology of Kalinga ceramic design.* Ph.D. dissertation, Department of Anthropology, University of Arizona, Tucson.
  1985   Ceramic design variation within a Kalinga village: Temporal and spatial processes. In *Decoding prehistoric ceramics,* edited by Ben Nelson, pp. 5-34. Southern Illinois University Press, Carbondale.
  1991   Pottery production and distribution among the Kalinga: A study of household and re-

gional organization and differentiation. In *Ceramic ethnoarchaeology,* edited by W. A. Longacre, pp. 112-143. University of Arizona Press, Tucson.

Griffiths, Dorothy M.
1978   Use-marks on historic ceramics: A preliminary study. *Historical Archaeology* 12:68-81.

Gunstone, Frank D., and Frank A. Norris
1983   *Lipids in foods: Chemistry, biochemistry and technology.* Pergamon Press, New York.

Hally, David J.
1983a   Use alteration of pottery vessel surfaces: An important source of evidence for the identification of vessel function. *North American Archaeologist* 4:3-26.
1983b   The interpretive potential of pottery from domestic contexts. *Midcontinental Journal of Archaeology* 8:163-196.
1986   The identification of vessel function: A case study from Northwest Georgia. *American Antiquity* 51:267-295.

Hastorf, C. A., and M. J. DeNiro
1985   Reconstruction of prehistoric plant production and cooking practices by a new isotopic method. *Nature* 315:489-491.

Hayden, Brian
1979   Snap, shatter, and superfracture: Use-wear of stone skin scrapers. In *Lithic use-wear analysis,* edited by B. Hayden, pp. 207-229. Academic Press, New York.

Hayden, Brian, and Aubrey Cannon
1983   Where the garbage goes: Refuse disposal in the Maya Highlands. *Journal of Anthropological Archaeology* 2:117-163.
1984   The structure of material systems: Ethnoarchaeology in the Maya Highlands. *Society for American Archaeology Papers No. 3,* Washington, D.C.

Henrickson, E. F.
1990   Investigating ancient ceramic form and use: Progress report and case study. In *The changing roles of ceramics in society: 26,000 B.P. to the present,* edited by W. D. Kingery, pp. 83-118. The American Ceramic Society, Westerville, Ohio.

Henrickson, E. F., and M. A. McDonald
1983   Ceramic form and function: An ethnographic search and archaeological application. *American Anthropologist* 85:630-643.

Heron, C., R. P. Evershed, L. J. Goad, and V. Denham
1991a   New approaches to the analysis of organic residues from archaeological remains. In *Proceedings of a conference on the application of scientific techniques to archaeology,* edited by P. Budd, B. Chapman, C. Jackson, R. Janaway, and B. Ottaway, pp. 332-339. *Oxbow Monograph 9.*

Heron, C., R. P. Evershed, and L. J. Goad
1991b   Effects of migration of soil lipids on organic residues associated with buried potsherds. *Journal of Archaeological Science* 18:641-659.

Hester, T. R., and R. F. Heizer
1973   Bibliography of archaeology 1: Experiments, lithic technology, and petrography. *Addison-Wesley Module in Anthropology* 29.

Hilditch, T. P., and P. N. Williams
1964   *The chemical constitution of natural fats.* John Wiley and Sons, New York.

Hill, H. E., and John Evans
1987   The identification of plants used in prehistory from organic residues. In *Archaeometry: Further Australian studies,* edited by W. R. Ambrose and J. M. J. Mummery, pp. 90-96. Department of Prehistory, Research School of Pacific Studies, Australian National University, Canberra.
1989   Crops of the Pacific: New evidence from chemical analysis of organic residues in pottery.

In *Foraging and farming: The evolution of plant exploitation,* edited by D. R. Harris and G. C. Hillman, pp. 418-425. Unwin Hyman, London.

Hill, H. E., J. Evans, and M. Card
1985   Organic residues on 3000 year old potsherds from Natunuku, Fiji. *New Zealand Journal of Archaeology* 7:125-128.

Hill, James N.
1970   Broken K Pueblo: Prehistoric social organization in the American Southwest. *Anthropological Papers of the University of Arizona 18.* University of Arizona Press, Tucson.

Hitchcock, C., and B. W. Nichols
1971   *Plant lipid biochemistry: The biochemistry of fatty acids and acyl lipids with particular reference to higher plants and algae.* Academic Press, New York.

Hodder, Ian
1982   *Symbols in action.* Cambridge University Press, New York.

Hodson, F. R.
1970   Cluster analysis and archaeology: Some new developments and applications. *World Archaeology* 20:61-70.

Howard, Hillary
1981   In the wake of distribution: Towards an integrated approach to ceramic studies in prehistoric Britain. In *Production and distribution: A ceramic viewpoint,* edited by H. Howard and E. L. Morris, pp. 1-30. British Archaeological Reports International Series 120, Oxford.

Huckell, Bruce B.
1979   Of chipped stone tools, elephants, and the Clovis hunters: An experiment. *Plains Anthropologist* 24:177-189.
1982   The Denver elephant project: A report on experimentation with thrusting spears. *Plains Anthropologist* 27:217-244.

Ingersoll, Daniel, John E. Yellen, and William McDonald
1977   Introduction. In *Experimental archaeology,* edited by D. Ingersoll, J. E. Yellen, and W. McDonald, pp. xi-xviii. Columbia University Press, New York.

James, Charles D., III, and Alexander J. Lindsay, Jr.
1973   Ethnoarchaeological research at Canyon del Muerto, Arizona: A Navajo example. *Ethnohistory* 20:361-374.

Jelinek, Arthur J.
1976   Form, function, and style in lithic analysis. In *Cultural change and continuity: Essays in honor of James Bennett Griffin,* edited by C. E. Cleland, pp. 19-33. Academic Press, New York.

Jewell, P. A., and G. W. Dimbleby
1966   The experimental earthwork on Overton Down, Wiltshire, England: The first four years. *Proceedings of the Prehistoric Society* 32:313-342.

Johnson, L. L.
1978   A history of flint-knapping experimentation. *Current Anthropology* 19:337-372.

Jones, Bruce A.
1989   Use-wear analysis of White Mountain Redwares at Grasshopper Pueblo. *The Kiva* 54:353-360.

Keeley, Lawrence, H.
1974   Technique and methodology in microwear studies: A critical review. *World Archaeology* 5:323-336.
1980   *Experimental determination of stone tool uses: A microwear analysis.* University of Chicago Press, Chicago.

Keesing, Felix M.
1962   *The ethnohistory of northern Luzon.* Stanford University Press, Stanford.

Keesing, Felix M., and M. Keesing
  1934   *Taming Philippine headhunters: A study of government and cultural change in northern Luzon.*
          George Allen and Unwin, London.

Kent, Susan
  1987   Understanding the use of space: An ethnoarchaeological approach. In *Method and theory for activity area research,* edited by S. Kent, pp. 1-60. Columbia University Press, New York.

Kingery, W. D.
  1989   Ceramic materials science in society. *Annual Review of Materials Science* 19:1-20.

Kleindienst, Maxine R., and Patty Jo Watson
  1956   "Action archaeology": The archaeology of a living community. *Anthropology Tomorrow* 5(1):75-78.

Kluckhohn, Clyde
  1940   The conceptual structure in Middle American studies. In *The Maya and their neighbors,* edited by C. L. Hay *et al.,* pp. 41-51. Appleton-Century, New York.

Kobayashi, Masashi
  n.d.   A study of cooking behavior: An ethnoarchaeological perspective. In *Kalinga ethnoarchaeology,* edited by W. A. Longacre and J. M. Skibo. Smithsonian Institution Press, Washington, D.C. (in press).

Kramer, Carol
  1979   An archaeological view of a contemporary Kurdish village: Domestic architecture, household size, and wealth. In *Ethnoarchaeology: Implications of ethnography for archaeology,* edited by C. Kramer, pp. 139-163. Columbia University Press, New York.

  1982   *Village ethnoarchaeology: Rural Iran in archaeological perspective.* Academic Press, New York.

  1985   Ceramic ethnoarchaeology. *Annual Review of Anthropology* 14:77-102.

Lancaster, Judith
  1986   Wind action on stone artifacts: An experiment in site modification. *Journal of Field Archaeology* 13:359-363.

Lawless, Robert
  1977   Societal ecology in northern Luzon: Kalinga agriculture, organization, population, and change. *University of Oklahoma Papers in Anthropology* 18:1-136.

Lewenstein, Suzanne M.
  1987   *Stone tool use at Cerros: The ethnoarchaeological and use-wear evidence.* University of Texas Press, Austin.

Linton, Ralph
  1944   North American cooking pots. *American Antiquity* 9:369-380.

Lischka, Joseph J.
  1978   A functional analysis of Middle Classic ceramics at Kaminaljuyu. In *The ceramics of Kaminaljuyu,* edited by R. K. Wetherington, pp. 223-278. Pennsylvania State University Press, University Park.

London, Gloria Anne
  1985   Decoding designs: The Late Third Millennium b.c. pottery from Jebel Qacaqir. Ph.D. dissertation, University of Arizona, Tucson.

Longacre, William A.
  1970   Archaeology as anthropology: A case study. *Anthropological papers of the University of Arizona 17.* University of Arizona Press, Tucson.

  1974   Kalinga pottery-making: The evolution of a research design. In *Frontiers of anthropology,* edited by Murray J. Leaf, pp. 51-67. D. Van Nostrand, New York.

  1981   Kalinga pottery: An ethnoarchaeological study. In *Patterns of the past: Studies in honour of*

David Clarke, edited by I. Hodder, G. Isaac, and N. Hammond, pp. 49-66. Cambridge University Press, London.

1985   Pottery use-life among the Kalinga, northern Luzon, the Philippines. In *Decoding prehistoric ceramics,* edited by Ben Nelson, pp. 334-346. Southern Illinois University Press, Carbondale.

1991a   Ceramic ethnoarchaeology: An introduction. In *Ceramic ethnoarchaeology,* edited by W. A. Longacre, pp. 1-10. University of Arizona Press, Tucson.

1991b   Sources of ceramic variability among the Kalinga of northern Luzon. In *Ceramic ethnoarchaeology,* edited by W. A. Longacre, pp. 95-111. University of Arizona Press, Tucson.

Longacre, William A., Kenneth L. Kvamme, and Masashi Kobayashi

1988   Southwestern pottery standardization: An ethnoarchaeological view from the Philippines. *The Kiva* 53:101-112.

Longacre, William A., and James M. Skibo (editors)

n.d.   *Kalinga ethnoarchaeology.* Smithsonian Institution Press, Washington, D.C. (in press).

Longacre, William A., James M. Skibo, and Miriam T. Stark

1991   Ethnoarchaeology at the top of the world: New ceramic studies among the Kalinga of Luzon. *Expedition* 33:2-15.

Mabry, Jonathan, James M. Skibo, Michael B. Schiffer, and Kenneth Kvamme

1988   Use of a falling-weight tester for assessing ceramic impact strength. *American Antiquity* 53:830-839.

Marchbanks, Michael Lee

1989   *Lipid analysis in archaeology: An initial study of ceramics and subsistence at the George C. Davis site.* Master's thesis, University of Texas at Austin.

Martin, Paul S.

1938   Archaeological work in the Ackmen-Lowry area, southwestern Colorado. *Archaeological Series 23(2),* Field Museum of Natural History, Chicago.

Matson, Fredrick R.

1965   Ceramic ecology: An approach to the study of early cultures of the Near East. In *Ceramics and man,* edited by F. R. Matson, pp. 202-218. Aldine Publishing, Chicago.

McPherron, Alan

1967   The Juntunen site and the Late Woodland prehistory of the Upper Great Lakes area. *Museum of Anthropology, University of Michigan Anthropological Papers 30.* Ann Arbor.

Medalia, Avrom I., and Donald Rivin

1982   Particulate carbon and other components of soot and carbon black. *Carbon* 20:481-492.

Mills, Barbara J.

1989   Integrating functional analyses of vessels and sherds through models of ceramic assemblage formation. *World Archaeology* 21:133-147.

Mindeleff, Cosmos

1896   Aboriginal remains in the Verde Valley, Arizona. *13th Annual Report of the Bureau of Ethnology, 1891-1892,* pp. 185-261. Smithsonian Institution Press, Washington, D.C.

Morgan, E. D., C. Conford, D. R. J. Pollock, and P. Isaacson

1973   The transformation of fatty materials buried in soil. *Science and Archaeology* 10:9-10.

Morgan, E. D., L. Titus, R. J. Small, and C. Edwards

1984   Gas chromatographic analysis of fatty material from a Tule midden. *Archaeometry* 26:43-48.

Morton, J. D., and H. P. Schwarcz

1988   Stable isotope analysis of food residues from Ontario ceramics. Paper presented at the 26th International Symposium of Archaeometry, Toronto.

Murray, Tim, and Michael J. Walker
  1988   Like what? A practical question of analogical inference and archaeological meaningfulness. *Journal of Anthropological Archaelogy* 7:248-287.

Nakano, Masuo
  1989a Recontruction of the ancient period by lipid analysis. In *What do new methods bring to the study of archaeology?* Committee of the University Science Symposium, pp. 114-131. Kubapuro Press, Tokyo (in Japanese).
  1989b Ancient lipids in archaeological remains. *The Quaternary Research* 28:337-340 (in Japanese).

Nelson, Ben A.
  1981   Ethnoarchaeology and paleodemography: A test of Turner and Lofgren's hypothesis. *Journal of Anthropological Research* 37:107-129.
  1991   Ceramic frequency and use-life: A Highland Mayan case in cross-cultural perspective. In *Ceramic ethnoarchaeology,* edited by W. A. Longacre, pp. 162-181. University of Arizona Press, Tucson.

Nelson, Ben A., and Steven A. LeBlanc
  1986   *Short-term sedentism in the American Southwest: The Mimbres Valley Salado.* Maxwell Museum of Anthropology, University of New Mexico Press, Albuquerque.

Neupert, Mark, and William A. Longacre
  n.d.   Informant accuracy in pottery use-life studies: A Kalinga example. In *Kalinga ethnoarchaeology,* edited by W. A. Longacre and J. M. Skibo. Smithsonian Institution Press, Washington, D.C. (in press).

Nicklin, Keith W.
  1981   Pottery production and distribution in southeast Nigeria. In *Production and distribution: A ceramic viewpoint,* edited by H. Howard and E. L. Morris, pp. 31-44. *British Archaeological Reports* 120, Oxford.

Nielsen, Axel E.
  1991   Trampling the archaeological record: An experimental study. *American Antiquity* 56:483-503.

O'Brien, Patrick
  1990   An experimental study of the effects of salt erosion on pottery. *Journal of Archaeological Science* 17:393-401.

Odell, George H., and Frank Cowan
  1986   Experiments with spears and arrows on animal targets. *Journal of Field Archaeology* 13:195-212.

Odell, George H., and F. Odell-Vereecken
  1980   Verifying reliability of lithic use-wear assessments by "blind tests": The low-power approach. *Journal of Field Archaeology* 7:87-120.

Oswalt, Wendell H.
  1974   Ethnoarchaeology. In *Ethnoarchaeology,* edited by C. B. Donnan and C. W. Clewlow, Jr., pp. 3-14. *Institute of Archaeology, Monograph IV,* University of California, Los Angeles.

Oswalt, Wendell H., and James W. VanStone
  1967   The ethnoarchaeology of Crow Village, Alaska. *Smithsonian Institution Bureau of American Ethnology Bulletin 199,* Washington, D.C.

Pastron, A. G.
  1974   Preliminary ethnoarchaeological investigations among the Tarahumara. In *Ethnoarchaeology,* edited by C. B. Donnan and C. W. Clewlow, Jr., pp. 93-114. *Institute of Archaeology, Monograph IV.* University of California, Los Angeles.

Patrick, M., A. J. deKoning, and A. B. Smith
  1985 Gas liquid chromatographic analysis of fatty acids in food residues from ceramic in the southwestern Cape, South Africa. *Archaeometry* 27:231-236.
Plog, Stephen
  1980 *Stylistic variation in prehistoric ceramics.* Cambridge University Press, New York.
  1985 Estimating vessel orifice diameters: Measurement methods and measurement error. In *Decoding prehistoric ceramics,* edited by B. A. Nelson, pp. 243-253. University of Illinois Press, Carbondale.
Rathje, William L.
  1990 Method, theory, and dirt: The Garbage Project at 17. Paper presented at the Society for American Archaeology Meetings, Las Vegas.
Rathje, William L., and Michael B. Schiffer
  1982 *Archaeology.* Harcourt Brace Jovanovich, New York.
Reid, J. Jefferson
  1973 Growth and response to stress at Grasshopper Pueblo, Arizona. Ph.D. dissertation, University of Arizona, Tucson.
Reid, J. Jefferson, Michael B. Schiffer, and William L. Rathje
  1975 Behavioral archaeology: Four strategies. *American Anthropologist* 77:864-869.
Reynolds, Barrie, and Margaret A. Scott (editors)
  1987 *Material anthropology: Contemporary approaches to material culture.* University Press of America, New York.
Rice, Prudence M.
  1987 *Pottery analysis: A sourcebook.* University of Chicago Press, Chicago.
  1990 Functions and uses of archaeological ceramics. In *The changing roles of ceramics in society: 26,000 B.P. to the present,* edited by W. D. Kingery, pp. 1-12. American Ceramic Society, Westerville, Ohio.
Richardson, Miles (editor)
  1974 *The human mirror: Material and spatial images of man.* Louisiana State University Press, Baton Rouge.
Rogers, Malcolm J.
  1936 Yuman pottery making. *San Diego Museum Papers 2,* San Diego.
Rottlander, Rolf C. A.
  1990 Lipid analysis in the identification of vessel contents. In *Organic contents of ancient vessels,* edited by W. R. Biers and P. E. McGovern, pp. 37-40. *MASCA Research Papers in Science and Archaeology, Vol. 7.* University of Pennsylvania, Philadelphia.
Rottlander, Rolf C. A., and H. Schlichtherle
  1978 Food identification of samples from archaeological sites. *Archaeo-Physika* 10:260-267.
  1983 Analysis of contents of prehistoric vessels. *Naturwissenschaften* 70:33-38 (in German).
Rye, Owen S.
  1981 *Pottery technology: Principles and reconstruction.* Taraxacum, Washington, D.C.
Sackett, James R.
  1977 The meaning of style in archaeology: A general framework. *American Antiquity* 42:369-380.
Sala, Irene Levi
  1986 Use wear and post-depositional surface modification: A word of caution. *Journal of Archaeological Science* 13:229-244.
Salls, Roy A.
  1985 The scraper plane: A functional interpretation. *Journal of Field Archaeology* 12:99-106.
Salmon, Merrilee H.
  1982 *Philosophy and archaeology.* Academic Press, New York.

Sassaman, Kenneth E.
1991   *Economic and social contexts of early ceramic vessel technology in the American Southeast.*
       Ph.D. dissertation, University of Massachusetts, Amherst.

Schiffer, Michael B.
n.d.   *Technological perspectives on behavioral change.* University of Arizona Press, Tucson (in
       press).
1972   Archaeological context and systemic context. *American Antiquity* 37:156-165.
1975   Behavioral chain analysis: Activities, organization, and the use of space. *Fieldiana: Anthro-
       pology* 65:103-119.
1976   *Behavioral archeology.* Academic Press, New York.
1978   Methodological issues in ethnoarchaeology. In *Explorations in ethnoarchaeology,* edited by
       R. A. Gould, pp. 229-247. University of New Mexico Press, Albuquerque.
1981   Some issues in the philosophy of archaeology. *American Antiquity* 46:899-908.
1987   *Formation processes of the archaeological record.* University of New Mexico Press,
       Albuquerque.
1988a The structure of archaeological theory. *American Antiquity* 53:461-485.
1988b The effects of surface treatment on permeability and evaporative cooling effectiveness of
       pottery. In *Proceedings of the 26th International Archaeometry Symposium,* edited by R. M.
       Farquhar, R. G. V. Hancock, and L. A. Pavlish, pp. 23-29. Archaeometry Laboratory, De-
       partment of Physics, University of Toronto, Toronto, Ontario.
1989   A research design for ceramic use-wear analysis at Grasshopper Pueblo. In *Pottery technol-
       ogy: Ideas and approaches,* edited by G. Bronitsky, pp. 183-205. Westview Press, Boulder,
       Colorado.
1990   The influence of surface treatment on heating effectiveness of ceramic vessels. *Journal of
       Archaeological Science* 17:373-381.

Schiffer, Michael B., and James M. Skibo
1987   Theory and experiment in the study of technological change. *Current Anthropology*
       28:595-622.
1989   A provisional theory of ceramic abrasion. *American Anthropologist* 91:102-116.

Semenov, Sergei A.
1964   *Prehistoric technology* (translated by M. W. Thompson). Cory, Adams and Mackay, London.

Shepard, Anna O.
1965   Ceramics for the archaeologist. *Carnegie Institution of Washington, Publication 609.*

Sinopoli, Carla M.
1991   *Approaches to archaeological ceramics.* Plenum Press, New York.

Skibo, James M.
n.d.   The Kalinga cooking pot: An ethnoarchaeological and experimental evaluation of perfor-
       mance characteristics. In *Kalinga ethnoarchaeology,* edited by W. A. Longacre and J. M.
       Skibo. Smithsonian Institution Press, Washington, D.C. (in press).
1987   Fluvial sherd abrasion and the interpretation of surface remains on Southwestern bajadas.
       North American Archaeologist 8:125-142.

Skibo, James M., and Michael B. Schiffer
1987   The effects of water on processes of ceramic abrasion. *Journal of Archaeological Science*
       14:83-96.

Skibo, James M., Michael B. Schiffer, and Kenneth C. Reid
1989a Organic-tempered pottery: An experimental study. *American Antiquity* 54:122-146.

Skibo, James M., Michael B. Schiffer, and Nancy Kowalski
1989b Ceramic style analysis in archaeology and ethnoarchaeology: Bridging the analytical gap.
       Journal of Anthropological Archaeology 8:388-409.

Smith, Marian J., Jr.
1983   *The study of ceramic function from artifact size and shape.* Ph.D. dissertation, Department of Anthropology, University of Oregon.
1985   Toward an economic interpretation of ceramics: Relating vessel size and shape to use. In *Decoding prehistoric ceramics,* edited by B. A. Nelson, pp. 254-309. Southern Illinois University Press, Carbondale.
1988   Function from whole vessel shape: A method and an application to Anasazi Black Mesa, Arizona. *American Anthropologist* 90:912-922.

Speth, John D.
1974   Experimental investigation of hard-hammer percussion flaking. *Tebiwa* 17:7-36.

Stanish, Charles
1989   Household archaeology: Testing models of zonal complementarity in the South Central Andes. *American Anthropologist* 91:7-24.

Stanislawski, Michael B.
1974   The relationships of ethnoarchaeology, traditional, and systems archaeology. In *Ethnoarchaeology,* edited by C. B. Donnan and C. W. Clewlow, Jr., pp. 15-26. *Institute of Archaeology Monograph 24,* University of California, Los Angeles.

Stark, Miriam T.
n.d.   Pottery exchange from an ethnoarchaeological perspective: A Kalinga case study. In *Kalinga ethnoarchaeology,* edited by W. A. Longacre and J. M. Skibo. Smithsonian Institution Press, Washington, D.C. (in press).
1991   Ceramic production and community specialization: A Kalinga ethnoarchaeological study. *World Archaeology* 23:64-78.

Staski, Edward
1991   Where and how the litterbug bites: Unauthorized refuse disposal in the late 19th century American cities. In *The ethnoarchaeology of refuse disposal,* edited by E. Staski and L. D. Sutro, pp. 33-39. *Anthropological Research Papers No. 42.* Arizona State University, Tempe.

Steponaitis, Vincas P.
1983   *Ceramics, chronology, and community patterns: An archaeological study at Moundville.* Academic Press, New York.

Steward, Julian H., and Frank M. Setzler
1938   Function and configuration in archaeology. *American Antiquity* 4:4-10.

Stiles, Daniel
1977   Ethnoarchaeology: A discussion of methods and applications. *Man* 12:87-103.

Stimmell, Carole, Robert B. Heimann, and R. G. V. Hancock
1982   Indian pottery from the Mississippi Valley: Coping with bad materials. In *Archaeological ceramics,* edited by J. S. Olin and A. D. Franklin, pp. 219-228. Smithsonian Institution Press, Washington, D.C.

Sullivan, Alan P., III
1978   Inference and evidence in archaeology: A discussion of the conceptual problems. In *Advances in archaeological method and theory,* Vol. 1, edited by M. B. Schiffer, pp. 183-222. Academic Press, New York.

Takaki, Michiko
1977   *Aspects of exchange in Kalinga society, northern Luzon.* Ph.D. dissertation, Yale University.

Tani, Masakazu
n.d.   Why should more pots break in larger households? Mechanisms underlying population estimates from ceramics. In *Kalinga ethnoarchaeology,* edited by W. A. Longacre and J. M. Skibo. Smithsonian Institution Press, Washington, D.C. (in press).

Tankersley, Ken, and John Meinhart
1982   Physical and structural properties of ceramic materials utilized by a Fort Ancient group. *Midcontinental Journal of Archaeology* 7:225-243.

Taylor, Walter W.
1983   *A study of archaeology.* Southern Illinois University Press, Carbondale.

Thompson, Raymond H.
1956   The subjective element in archaeological inference. *Southwestern Journal of Anthropology* 12:327-332.
1958   Modern Yucatecan Mayan pottery making. *Memoirs of the Society for American Archaeology* 15. Society for American Archaeology, Salt Lake City.
1991   The archaeological purpose of ethnoarchaeology. In *Ceramic ethnoarchaeology,* edited by W. A. Longacre, pp. 231-245. University of Arizona Press, Tucson.

Thorton, M. D., E. D. Morgan, and F. Celoria
1970   The composition of bog butter. *Science and Archaeology* 2/3:20-25.

Tillman, David A.
1978   *Wood as an energy resource.* Academic Press, New York.

Tillman, David A., Amadeo J. Rossi, and William D. Kitto
1981   *Wood combustion: Principles, processes, and economics.* Academic Press, New York.

Tringham, Ruth
1978   Experimentation, ethnoarchaeology, and leapfrogs in archaeological methodology. In *Explorations in ethnoarchaeology,* edited by R. A. Gould, pp. 169-199. University of New Mexico Press, Albuquerque.

Tringham, Ruth, Glenn Cooper, George Odell, Barbara Voytek, and Anne Whitman
1974   Experimentation in the formation of edge damage: A new approach to lithic analysis. *Journal of Field Archaeology* 1:171-196.

Trostel, Brian
n.d.   A comparison of household wealth and ceramic variables in a Kalinga village. In *Kalinga ethnoarchaeology,* edited by W. A. Longacre and J. M. Skibo. Smithsonian Institution Press, Washington, D.C. (in press).

Turner, Christy G., II, and Laurel Lofgren
1966   Household size of prehistoric Western Pueblo Indians. *Southwestern Journal of Anthropology* 22:117-132.

Upham, Steadman
1982   *Polities and power: An economic and political history of the Western Pueblo.* Academic Press, New York.

Vaughan, Patrick
1985   *Use-wear analysis of flaked stone tools.* University of Arizona Press, Tucson.

Vaz Pinto, Ines, Michael B. Schiffer, Susan Smith, and James M. Skibo
1987   Effects of temper on ceramic abrasion resistance: A preliminary investigation. *Archaeomaterials* 1:119-134.

Villa, P., and J. Courtin
1983   The interpretation of stratified sites: A view from underground. *Journal of Archaeological Science* 10:267-281.

Vitelli, Karen D.
1984   Greek Neolithic pottery by experiment. In *Pots and potters,* edited by P. Rice, pp. 113-131. *Institute of Archaeology, Monograph XXIV,* University of California, Los Angeles.

Watson, Patty Jo
1979   Archaeological ethnography in western Iran. *Viking Fund Publication in Anthropology No. 57.* University of Arizona Press, Tucson.
1982   Review of *Living archaeology* by R. A. Gould. *American Antiquity* 47:445-448.

1983   Foreword to the 1983 edition, *A study of archaeology,* by W. W. Taylor, pp. ix-xvi. Southern Illinois University Press, Carbondale.

Wilk, Richard R., and William L. Rathje (editors)

1982   Household archaeology: Building a prehistory of domestic life. *American Behavioral Scientist* 25(6).

Willey, Gordon R., and Jeremy A. Sabloff

1980   *A history of American archaeology.* W. H. Freeman, San Francisco.

Wilson, Douglas C., William L. Rathje, and Wilson W. Hughes

1991   Household discards and modern refuse: A principle of household resource use and waste. In *The ethnoarchaeology of refuse disposal,* edited by E. Staski and L. D. Sutro, pp. 41-51. *Anthropological Research Papers No. 42.* Arizona State University, Tempe.

Wylie, Alison

1982   An analogy by another name is just as anological. A commentary on the Gould-Watson dialogue. *Journal of Anthropological Archaeology* 1:382-401.

1985   The reaction against analogy. In *Advances in archaeological method and theory,* edited by M. B. Schiffer, pp. 63-111. Academic Press, New York.

Yellen, John E.

1977   *Archaeological approaches to the present: Models for reconstructing the past.* Academic Press, New York.

Young, Lisa C., and Tammy Stone

1990   The thermal properties of textured ceramics: An experimental study. *Journal of Field Archaeology* 17:195-203.

Index